Reading Sexualities

D1809160

Reading Sexualities confronts the reigning practices, priorities, and pre-occupations of queer theory and sexuality studies. Looking at a range of texts, from novels to travel narratives to internet porn, Donald E. Hall deftly weaves the theoretical with the literary to:

- examine the vexed ethical, critical, and political questions arising from sexual consumerism and cross-cultural encounters;
- read the changing landscape of sexual identity, finding great cause for optimism and enthusiastic engagement;
- urge readers to embrace a far-reaching dialogic practice as a mechanism for furthering radical social change.

Reading Sexualities shows how our sexual desires and bases for identification are being widely challenged and changed. Drawing on herme-neutic theory and the work of Hans-Georg Gadamer, Hall argues that by approaching sexual diversity with openness and humility we become active participants in the politically urgent process of reading the self through the perspective of the other.

Donald E. Hall is Jackson Distinguished Professor of English and Chair of the Department of English at West Virginia University. He is a long-time political activist and the author or editor of nine previous books in the fields of gender studies, higher education studies, and Victorian studies. These include *Fixing Patriarchy, RePresenting Bisexualities, Queer Theories,* and *Subjectivity.*

Reading Sexualities

Hermeneutic theory and the future of
queer studies

Donald E. Hall

 Routledge
Taylor & Francis Group

LONDON AND NEW YORK

First published 2009
by Routledge
2 Park Square, Milton Park, Abingdon OX14 4RN

Simultaneously published in the USA and Canada
by Routledge
270 Madison Ave, New York, NY 10016

Routledge is an imprint of the Taylor & Francis Group, an informa business

Typeset in Sabon by
Taylor & Francis Books
Printed and bound in Great Britain by
TJ International Ltd, Padstow, Cornwall

British Library Cataloguing in Publication Data
A catalogue record for this book is available from the British Library

Library of Congress Cataloging in Publication Data
Reading sexualities: hermeneutic theory and the future of queer studies /
Donald E. Hall. – 1st ed.
       p. cm.
   Includes bibliographical references and index.
   1. Homosexuality in literature. 2. Homosexuality and literature. 3.
Homosexuality – Philosophy. 4. Gays – Identity. 5. Gay and lesbian studies. 6.
Queer theory. 7. Hermeneutics. 8. Phenomenology and literature. I. Title.
   PN56.H57H36 2009
   809.' 93352664 – dc22
                              2008047757

ISBN10: 0-415-36785-9 (hbk)   ISBN13: 978-0-415-36785-1 (hbk)
ISBN10: 0-415-36786-7 (pbk)   ISBN13: 978-0-415-36786-8 (pbk)
ISBN10: 0-203-02026-X (ebk)   ISBN13: 978-0-203-02026-5 (ebk)

Contents

Acknowledgments

This book has been the product of many years of discussion, research, and life experience. First and foremost, I want to thank my colleagues at California State University, Northridge (CSUN), and West Virginia University (WVU) who have provided exceptional intellectual, professional, and personal support. Without all of you, this book would have been impossible.

Just as influential have been the students that I have taught over the thirteen years I spent at CSUN and my five years at WVU. I owe you all a debt of thanks for continuing to teach me about your lives and perspectives. Additionally, students in queer studies seminars that I taught at the University of Graz, the University of Helsinki, the University of Malmö, and the University of Szeged offered key insights on the global reach and limitations of queer studies.

I owe sincere thanks to my research assistants at WVU: Robert Fanning, Lumi Dragulescu, Jessica Queener, and especially Andrew Urban. Andrew read this manuscript many times and made invaluable suggestions.

I appreciate the generosity of the journal *Nineteenth-Century Prose* and its Editor Barry Tharaud for allowing me to reprint key passages and insights in my fifth chapter here that are drawn from an essay ("Body Fluid Desire") that first appeared in *NCP* 26.1 (1999).

Finally, I am indebted deeply to Bill Maruyama who has joined me on this queer adventure in life. His horizon has changed mine forever.

I dedicate this book to Bill and everyone else who has been tempted to leave behind the safe and familiar...and then did.

Introduction

Sexual identity is a narrative we tell ourselves and we tell about ourselves. We choose (and, to varying extents, have chosen for us) a set of primary identifiers from a myriad of fleeting and sustained desires that we feel over a lifetime and even the course of an eventful day. Sizes, shapes, body contours, genitalia, smells, skin textures, skin colors, pitches of voice, arches of feet—any of these may or may not elicit a response classifiable as "sexual" or "erotic," and carry considerable, some, or no amount of weight in our personal physics of primary, secondary, and unimportant sexual identity components. "I am a..." follows from a set of decisions and impositions that reduces the uncapturable complexity of our sensual and emotional responses to a convenient story and history that, more often than not, fits within the taxonomy provided by late-nineteenth-century sexology and the identity politics that followed from it. Michel Foucault, as oversimplifying as he often is, points accurately to that newly narrative quality of sexual identity when he says the "nineteenth-century homosexual became a personage, a past, a case history, a childhood, in addition to being a type of life, a life form, and a morphology" (Foucault 1990: 43). Of course, this is true not only for the "homosexual." The flagellist, the exhibitionist, the voyeur, and even the "queer" all have their own narrative trajectory, even as the binary of hetero/homo tends to overwrite most other classifications.

As obvious as this may seem, I contend that sexuality studies has yet to grapple forthrightly with the reductive and seductive ways that narratives constitute sexual identity. We read and write about sex and sexuality, about others' practices and about our own identities, yet there is no specifically sexual narratology. And that is only one of several omissions that await attention from theoreticians working in the field. For example, Sara Ahmed's insightful *Queer Phenomenology* (2006) does not, in fact, explore the phenomenology of our processing and categorizing of desire. A queer phenomenology could attempt a thick description of a single stroll down a crowded street, an afternoon's passionate encounter, a viewing of an erotic film, a traversing of a room filled with strangers, or a visit to an art gallery. All of those occasions (along with innumerable others) demand of us a sorting out of phenomena, a careful acknowledgment and selection of responses, a privileging of some and denial of others, and a hierarchizing of the central and the peripheral that allows us to maintain the always threatened construct that is a unified "sexual identity" (though admittedly, those are hardly all conscious processes, as I will explore later). Even what we call the "sexual" rather than the aesthetic, the emotional, the friendly, or the enviable is so bound up in our fictions of a monolithic identity that one can hardly fault Ahmed and others for shying away from the project of a brash, descriptive phenomenology of desire.

Nor is that my exact project here though it will surface at times like the inevitable return of the repressed. Rather, I want to treat our sexual narratives as occasions for reading and, more to the point, readerly response. We have a wide variety of theories attempting to explain how and from where our senses of self arise and the ways those selves are then expressed socially and culturally: Explorations of discourse, ideology, and performance are all ways of theorizing the narratives that we inhabit and that inhabit us. Those theoretical tools and the investments they require are also narratives that work on us, even as we work with and sometimes against them. Like sexual identity, theoretical identity is both reductive and seductive, a necessary fiction and also a trap that deserves a good struggle. These are not separate topics. An over-arching question here will be: To what extent does the processing of narratives of theory, fiction, or nonfiction affect or infect our narratives of sexual self-understanding? Can reading queer us?

Two texts about reading

In the second vignette from Roger Earl's 1986 video release *Bi-Ceps: An Incredible Bisexual Experience,* Sheila and two of her male classmates from "night school" are reading over their notes for a psychology exam. After Sheila answers a call from her roommate Betty Jo (who, in Scene 1, was shown having sex with two brothers and then ridiculing their timidity until they had sex with each other), one of the classmates comments archly that Betty Jo is probably out that night "trying to prove all of Freud's theories on human sexuality." Sheila replies, "Listen smart ass, sometimes you can learn a lot more by *doing* than by just sitting around and *reading* about it out of some book." The other guy agrees, "I say let's dump the books and get down to practicing the theory....We've got to try things; if we don't experiment, we're going to miss out on some of the things life has to offer. To quote Auntie Mame, 'Life is a banquet and most poor sons of bitches are starving to death'."

Needless to say, no one goes hungry in the scene that follows. All sorts of imaginative sexual practices—with instant erections and exuberant orgasms easily achieved—follow seamlessly upon their decision to put into practice a motivating and (in their reading) fully supportive Freudian and Mamian theory base.

From a 2006 article on Deep Springs College, an isolated, all-male liberal arts institution in the high desert of California:

> Deep Spring's form of repression—its all-male self-enclosure—allows its students to feel wildly, hedonically free. Sometimes they make themselves a little hut and go live alone, or they take up apiculture or paint their toenails. They build things, break things, play pranks, hike naked, seduce (or try to seduce) female faculty. "Two guys had been reading a lot of queer theory—it was the nineties—and there was some fairly persuasive talk of a homosexual continuum," a Deep Springer told me. "These two guys more or less argued themselves, on a strictly theoretical basis, into making out. It was not the practical success that it had been theoretically. You can read all the Eve Kosofsky Sedgwick you want without getting an erection."
>
> (Goodyear 2006: 69)

How do we read these two texts? Of course, they are narratives relying upon memories or translations of the visual and aural into print representations that at once obscure and highlight, that are suspect and make any knowledge of fact impossible. Yet that mediation and imperfection does not forestall interpretation and a striving to understand, rather the opposite: it provides the very reason for the broadly cast conversation—the intellectual work—that is cultural studies. The irresolvably complex nature of texts is precisely why they are important as objects of scrutiny; their imperfections and mediations are those of our own mode of living. Their narratives are ours.

The lines among the "factual," the "theoretical," and the "fictional" can be blurry at times. The porn utopia of the "fictional" first scene above is clearly belied by the bodily failure of the "factual" second scene, though the two are linked in their initial optimism. In fact, that narrative idea/ideal of an easy translation of sexual theory (of whatever pedigree) into bodily practice through a simple decision-making process has become relatively common in the past few decades. This is the case not only in gay, heterosexual, and bisexual porn, but also in a host of other pop-cultural representations: in many episodes of *The Simpsons* (where the "homersexual" threat, in one episode's terminology, is so palpable because it is always there as a path of possible choice—"Well, I'll need some beer," is Homer's response to what he thinks is a sexual advance by Mr. Burns), in lyrics and print texts by Marilyn Manson (whose 1998 autobiography, *The Long Hard Road Out of Hell,* suggests that one can make oneself "gay" by following a few simple steps), and in erotic self-help books such as Annie Sprinkle's *Dr. Sprinkle's Spectacular Sex* and Susie Bright's *Full Exposure* (which I will discuss in Chapter 2). The conjoined limitations of and opportunities for self-directed instrumentality are further revealed and complicated in web-based interactions and explorations, in which a myriad of erotic options are easily accessible (a topic receiving attention in my conclusion). I would argue that our fascination with instrumentality also helps explain the explosive success of Viagra when it appeared on the market in 1998 and which promised new forms of erotic agency by way of a decision to "visit your doctor" and "ask him about" its effects, ones which may not have involved same-sex experimentation, but certainly the establishment or re-establishment of greater sexual freedom of choice (in fact, if the Deep Springs students above had had access to 10mg of "V" and used some porn to turn themselves on, they probably could have imperfectly consummated their theoretical desires for each other...where there is a will, there is often a circuitous way).

Popular culture is not alone in such musings. Instrumentality was key to some manifestations of 1970s and 1980s feminism that suggested feminism was the "theory" and lesbian sexuality the "practice" that should or could seamlessly follow (Annamarie Jagose in *Queer Theory: An Introduction* and Linda Garber in *Identity Poetics* have examined those claims with great insight). Finally, the erotic utopianism of *Bi-Ceps* and the other texts above has been reflected also in recent sociological theory, in works such as Ulrich Beck and Elisabeth Beck-Gernsheim's *The Normal Chaos of Love* from 1995 and Anthony Giddens's *The Transformation of Intimacy: Sexuality, Love and Eroticism in Modern Societies* from 1992. The former, while heavily footnoted, reads at times much like an erotic self-help book, even if it is a more conservative one than any by Bright or Sprinkle, in its implicit nostalgia for the days of stable heterosexual, nuclear families, and as it explores the "difficulties [that] lie in the principle of [erotic] free choice, which offers us new scope but also lands us with the responsibility for the results, good or bad" (Beck-Gernsheim 1995: 79).

Giddens's *Transformation of Intimacy* is similar, though certainly more celebratory in its exploration of "plastic sexuality, severed from its age-old integration with reproduction" (Giddens 1992: 27). "Plastic sexuality," Giddens suggests, "has its origins in the tendency, initiated somewhere in the late eighteenth century, strictly to limit family size; but it [now] [...] can be moulded as a trait of personality and thus is intrinsically bound up with the self" (1992: 2). For Giddens, sexuality is one of many such "moldable" aspects of the modern "self" as a thoroughly "reflexive project—a more or less continuous interrogation of past, present and future" (1992: 30). He asserts, "A person [now] 'has' a sexuality, gay or otherwise, which can be reflexively grasped, interrogated and developed" (1992: 14). He continues, "It is something each of us [...] cultivates, no longer a natural condition which an individual accepts as a preordained state of affairs. [...S]exuality [now] functions as a malleable feature of self" (1992: 15).

That broad and optimistic statement does capture a certain post-1960s narrative of erotic liberation, one that, however much Foucauldian skepticism we might bring to discussing it, still carries considerable, seductive appeal. Yet as many of us have discovered—inhabiting bodies that read and intellectually process but do not seamlessly incorporate that with which they agree politically or philosophically—the movement from theory to bodily practice is no simple step (and even the metaphor of a "step" implies a corporeal instrumentality that is highly problematic). Certainly, the students of Deep Springs College found that sexuality, whatever one's theory base, does not function as an easily malleable feature of selfhood. If they had read a little French narratology along with their queer theory, they might have run across Paul Ricoeur's reminder that we can become the "*narrator of our own story* without completely becoming the author of our life" (Ricoeur 1991c: 437, original italics).

Philosophers have long recognized that no aspect of selfhood is ever fully "mold-able," to use Giddens's term, in the way that one would work a piece of clay into a sculpture or shape liquid Jello into a dessert. As I explore more fully in *Subjectivity* (Hall 2004), this tantalizing question of instrumental agency over selfhood, its possibilities and stark limitations, was grappled with for centuries before Auntie Mame told us simply to *decide* to eat at the banquet of life, and by a host of commentators who may never have thought of extending their critique to the study of erotic behavior. It is a conversation that began at least as far back as the seventeenth century, with René Descartes and John Locke. As Charles Taylor argues in his *Sources of the Self: The Making of the Modern Identity*:

> What one finds running [though both Descartes and Locke] is the growing ideal of a human agent who is able to remake himself by methodical and disciplined action. What this calls for is the ability

to take an instrumental stance to one's given properties, desires, inclinations, tendencies, habits of thought and feeling, so that they can be *worked on,* doing away with some and strengthening others, until one meets the desired specifications. [...] Descartes's picture of the disengaged subject articulates the understanding of agency which is most congenial to this whole movement [and that] develops to its full form through Locke and the Enlightenment thinkers he influenced. [...] The key to this figure is that it gains control through disengagement. Disengagement is always correlative of an "objectification." [...] Objectifying a given domain involves depriving it of its normative force for us.

(Taylor 1989: 159–60)

Taylor goes on to demonstrate that the elusive ideal of "instrumentality" underlies much of modern science, economics, and theories of government (of self and others). As revealed above, it even provides a narrative base to today's pornography and erotic self-help books. Its critics point out, of course, that it can tend as well toward a particularly destructive solipsism, with Elizabeth Grosz noting in her discussion of mind/body dualism that "[s]ince the time of Descartes, not only is consciousness positioned outside of the world, outside its body, outside of nature; it is also removed from direct contact with other minds and a sociocultural community. At its extreme, all that consciousness can be sure about is its own existence" (1994: 7). Such insularity, I argue throughout this book, also threatens to render sterile, static, and wholly ineffective the work of those of us in queer studies, arch skeptics of Enlightenment-based philosophy, unless we too commit to direct and energetic contact with a broad sociocultural community.

Even as we decry its worst implications, we should remember that formulaic instrumentality through such outside positioning was always a highly questionable proposition, including among the philosophers of the Enlightenment. Locke, in his 1690 *An Essay Concerning Human Understanding,* argues that before executing any action that follows upon a desire, we have the power to suspend temporarily that execution, and "during this *suspension* [...] before the *will* be determined to action, and the action (which follows the determination) be done, we have the opportunity to examine, view, and judge, of the good or evil of what we are going to do" (Locke 1975: 263–4). Locke notes that we thereby have the ability to stop ourselves from doing what we might otherwise desire to do, and out of that ability comes our responsibility for ethical behavior. Nowhere, however, does Locke imply that we have an instrumental ability to create entirely *new* or different desires in ourselves. He even calls it "absurd" to imagine that one can "*will* [...] to be pleased with what [one] is pleased with" (1975: 247), or by implication at least, to will oneself into different pleasures.

E. J. Lowe sums up the limitations on self-directed change in noting that Locke "does not allow for the possibility of second-order volitions, strictly speaking: we cannot *will to will*" (1995: 135), or, I would add, *will to desire*. To whatever extent we can (and at times *must*) suspend our execution of desires, we cannot create new desires instrumentally, as the Deep Springers found out. Yes, we can strategize to create conditions under which our desire for a desire might lead to a form of approximately successful behavior (taking Viagra and watching porn to allow one to consummate an otherwise undesirable union), and we certainly can find ourselves altered over time through a wide variety of external forces and internal decision-making processes, as I explore throughout the coming pages. However, our sexualities are not mechanically controllable. The same limit on second-order volition is the basis also of some of the most incisive rejoinders to Giddens's work. Stjepan Meštrović argues that Giddens "ends up offering a caricature of the human agent [...] a portrait [...] based on oversimplified wishful thinking" (Meštrović 1998: 78); Giddens never acknowledges that while "human agents do create knowledgeable and meaningful representations of the world in the quest for what might be termed agency [...] they are also driven by powerful and mysterious passions" (1992: 49–50), ones that fall outside of any simple, instrumental *or* second-order volitional control.

The questions that I am raising here about instrumentality and selfhood have obvious implications for sexuality studies and a host of sexual-identity political issues, including reparative therapies and our basic terminology of "lifestyle" or "orientation." In struggling over and perhaps even embracing the possibility of some form of control over sexual selfhood, sexual nonconformists are certainly opening up a discursive space for reactionaries to call for them to take an objective stance toward, and commit to repudiating, their deviant desires and lifestyle. Whatever it takes, create in yourself "normal" and "natural" desires, some commentators would surely insist. Yet, at the same time, a widely circulating narrative of and belief in a degree of erotic instrumentality and "free choice" (as Ulrich Beck and Elisabeth Beck-Gernsheim term it) raises also all the temptations implied in *Bi-Ceps*. Rarely would people choose *not* to eat at a banquet if given a free meal ticket or, to put it another way, rarely would they decide upon the most repetitious set of performances if performative freedom is conceivable and, in terms of sexual exploration, disconnected to traditional narratives of reproductive and religious propriety. That was the queer motivation behind the Deep

Springs College students' actions, however disappointing the results. And, to my mind, praxis is always a laudable, if also always elusive goal.

It is also conceivable that I am giving those young men dabbling in queer sex a bit too much intellectual credit. Many commentators, including Giddens, have pointed out that we live in a consumer culture today that runs on narratives of newness and difference, on an engine of constant experimentation and the "trying on" of different identities as fashion items. As I argued in *Queer Theories* (Hall 2003), the quasi-commodification of queerness and sexual transgression proliferates but also politically dilutes the socially transformative, radical implications of "queer theory," especially in any ties it might retain to class-based analysis and social change. But here and in coming chapters I want neither simply to condemn nor celebrate this mythos, even as I return again to the fact that we actually do not and cannot change our sexuality as easily as we might dramatically alter our appearance with a new piercing, hair color, collagen injection, or nose job. In fact, the obsession with simply purchasing difference (and "improvement") may well derive from the frustrations we encounter in seeking change through much more elusive behavioral, attitudinal, and other forms of praxis-based work.

Thus, throughout my interrelated projects on "subjectivity," including my work on academic selfhood, I never want to be read as suggesting that there is anything simply or fundamentally wrong with narratives of self-directed agency—which Meštrović, in his response to Giddens, repeatedly condemns as a violent modernist project for mastery over selfhood and its surrounding world. On the contrary, I believe that grappling with agency, its possibilities and limitations, is the only way of honestly addressing how to hold ourselves responsible for *will*ful violence and degradation, as well as our complicities with the voracious, capitalist engine of consumption. The elusive quest for self-directed agency motivates; it excites; it energizes political, personal, and social transformation. It is the basis for what I would consider an ethical and responsible life. If we cannot continue to sort out where and to what extent we do have the ability to stop ourselves from doing that which we desire and to cultivate in ourselves (and others) new and different desires, I don't see how we can honestly address issues as varied as sexual violence, drug-related crimes, and the destruction of our natural world through our obsession with gas-guzzling vehicles and all encompassing disposability. I would love to see more people attempt to "will to will" to be more ethical and responsible community members, recognizing the contested nature of definitions of "ethical and responsible" behavior. And, frankly, I wouldn't mind seeing more people attempt to expand their sexual repertoire and responsiveness so that the violence-

producing polarities of hetero/homo are brashly, behaviorally decon-
structed. I would add, however, that in continuing to strive for such
instrumentality what we always risk is that our inevitable failure to
achieve simple and immediate instrumental control, or easy second-order
volition, can lead to cynicism, frustration, and resignation, over our
"selves" and our desires, as well as those of others.

That brings me to sexuality studies as it too has developed over the
past two decades. I will argue throughout this book that it is imperative
that we sexual radicals, queer theorists, and otherwise audacious iconoclasts continue to test and critically probe narratives of instrumentality,
even with and through the experience of failure, and that "queer" self-
identity, if that term is to retain any value, should involve an ongoing
project of enthusiastically politicized *hermeneutic* questioning.

The "queer" text

It is a well-known story but one worth retelling here. "Queer theory" burst
onto the scene almost two decades ago. The term received its first high-
profile usage in a special issue of the journal *differences* ("Queer Theory:
Lesbian and Gay Sexualities") published in the summer of 1991, was
mentioned in the same year in Diana Fuss's groundbreaking collection of
essays *Inside/Out,* and then gained wide notice with the publication in
1993 of Michael Warner's influential collection *Fear of a Queer Planet.*
By fall of 1993, I was teaching a queer-studies course at California State
University, Northridge, a class filled to capacity with politically agitated
students, many of whom were members of the campus activist group
SQUISH—Strong Queers United in Suppressing Heterosexism.

Since then, my classes, even in West Virginia where I now teach, have
always remained well enrolled (I often have to turn away students trying
to add, even with an enrollment cap of forty), but the political energy
has certainly diminished. There are many social contextual factors that
help explain this dissipation of fervor. Years of Bush administration lies
and media complicity sapped or squelched thoroughly the political energies of many of us. Furthermore, no one in my recent queer studies class
had known a single person who had died of AIDS, the seemingly
uncontrollable nature of which motivated much of the early energy in
queer activism. Since most of my undergraduates were born in the late
1980s and became sexually and socially self-aware in the past ten years,
they have never thought of AIDS as anything other than a pharmacolo-
gically managable disease (even if that is a very dangerous assumption).
And finally, compared to the early 1990s, media now provides forms of
modest and easily accessible validation. Ellen Degeneres's character on

her show *Ellen* came out on national television in 1997, and the series *Will and Grace* premiered in 1998, when most of my students were still in elementary school. Today, anyone who purchases expanded cable programming in West Virginia receives the gay/lesbian channel Logo, with its round-the-clock queer-marketed entertainment and advertising.

To be sure, my undergraduates still respond with great enthusiasm to many of the readings in the class, and especially to the early work of Judith Butler. Butler's implication of individual agency in changing sexual and gender norms through disruptive performances still makes us leave the classroom thinking that we can change the world if we first work creatively on ourselves or our "selves" (though I am hardly expecting students to read Butler and then try to Deep Spring each other). She proffers the possibility of a seductive, though elusive, instrumentality. Unfortunately, more recent theoretical work is often unhelpful in deepening the enthusiasm and sense of political attachment.

In fact, Teresa de Lauretis, one of the theorists who helped coin the phrase "queer theory" in the early 1990s, was quick to repudiate it just three years later, dismissing it as a "conceptually vacuous creature of the publishing industry" (de Lauretis 1994: 297). I found—and still find—that an over-hasty abandonment. Terms will always be appropriated, used differently, and even misused by the industries connected with the academy, and also by pop culture in general; such activity could be seen as a sign of vibrancy rather than failure. Yet I will grant de Lauretis one broad point: that something did change in the political energy that enlivened early queer studies. Contexts changed, but so did the priorities of those in the field, and some academic practitioners have become much more fundamentally disengaged than most of my students are.

Lee Edelman's *No Future: Queer Theory and the Death Drive* from 2004 is an oft-discussed case in point. Drawing on Lacanian theory, Edelman argues that queers should repudiate the "oppressively political" (Edelman 2004: 2), and abandon any claim to "a viable political future" (2004: 4). Edelman urges us to assert "that we do not intend a new politics, a better society, a brighter tomorrow, since all these fantasies reproduce the past, through displacement, in the form of the future" (2004: 31). What we embrace instead is "irony," which he calls the "queerest of rhetorical devices" (2004: 23). In his reading, however, irony is not a set of sustained articulations (a rhetoric-producing device); it can't be since it opposes "the very logic of making sense" (2004: 24). Over the course of the book, he does point to an acidic rejoinder or two as evidence of "explosive" queer irony (2004: 31); however, Edelmanian irony is primarily a type of gaze or attitude, one "uncannily returned by queers" to the heteronormative culture which had previously "displace[d it] onto the figure of the queer" (2004: 24). Apparently, *No Future* would have us roll our eyes and shoot withering looks at even the most virulent homophobes before quickly getting on with our apolitical queer lives. What should constitute those lives remains unnamed by Edelman (though since the bulk of his book involves readings of Hitchcock films, movie-watching is obviously part of an apolitical life). Given that Edelman is a successful academic, administrator, and lecturer, I would assume that his apolitical queer life would also encompass contributing to a retirement plan, helping students complete dissertations and strategize to finding job, and projecting forward to meet publication and other deadlines, all of which are heavily invested in the very "future" that he dismisses. "No future" may be a catchy slogan, but José Muñoz is actually generous in terming it "an easy move" and only the most spectacular of many recent "failures of imagination" (Muñoz 2006: 825, 826). I would go further and call it cynical and solipsistic.

Yet Edelman is not alone in repudiating the need for explicit projections concerning what "should be." Janet Halley and Andrew Parker have noted accurately that "the authors around whom queer theory crystallized seem to have spent the past decade distancing themselves from *their* previous work" (Halley and Parker 2007: 421–2). As I just mentioned, Judith Butler's work was integral to the fervor and iconoclasm of the early 1990s queer intellectual scene. Nothing was and is more energizing than the last eight pages of *Gender Trouble,* a conclusion entitled "From Parody to Politics." In it, Butler argues famously that the specific critical and political task that her politically engaged readers should assume is to locate sites for subversion, "to affirm the local possibilities of intervention through participating in precisely those practices of repetition that constitute identity and, therefore, present the immanent possibility of contesting them" (Butler 1999: 188). She issued a call to arms, suggesting that gender parodies (such as drag) and other disruptive social performances might work to create a better world for queers:

> If identities were no longer fixed as the premises of a political syllogism, and politics no longer understood as a set of practices derived from the alleged interests that belong to a set of ready-made subjects, a new configuration of politics would surely emerge from the ruins of the old.
>
> (Butler 1999: 189–90)

It is hardly surprising that the book was taken up by social-action groups such as Queer Nation. Love it or hate it, *Gender Trouble* stirred up readers by imagining a better future and offering a strategy to get there.

Butler backtracked quickly from those dynamic injunctions. Within three years, in *Bodies That Matter,* she made clear her belief that gender parody was not necessarily or even commonly political (Butler 1993: 125). In her more recent work *Undoing Gender,* she says that she probably wrote "From Parody to Politics" "too quickly," and that she only used drag parody as an instance in which the "differential effect of ontological presuppositions on the embodied life of individuals" is revealed to be "at work [... and] open to rearticulation" (Butler 2004: 213–14). She does not repudiate politics, as Edelman does, but certainly avoids articulating a specific tactic to replace her previous reliance on parody as action plan. She notes the need for a "radical democratic theory and practice that seeks to extend the norms that sustain viable life to previously disenfranchised communities" (2004: 225), but what that theory and practice might look like and how we might bring about change remain wholly unspecified.

As I will argue throughout this book, we desperately need an approach to sexual identity that motivates, that embraces the "politics" in identity politics, and that articulates a vision for the future. However, what made the early Butler so problematic was her implication of quick and thorough change, her rhetoric of "ruins" out of which new configurations would "surely" emerge. Sociopolitical change, sexual cultural change, and even self-directed change are hardly so cut-and-dried. We have seen some significant alterations in the past decade and more: the striking down of sodomy laws in the USA, the proliferation of lesbian and gay characters in the media, and the continuing decline of support among the young for discriminatory policies. Even so, nothing was shattered, and nothing new emerged out of any ruins. All these changes involved incremental additions or subtractions to law and public discourse. Even 9/11—the one event that is commonly figured as a social shattering—did not function in that way; it only led to a renewal and redirection of bombastic Cold War-style rhetoric and revival of longstanding, if sometimes submerged, xenophobia.

The origins of that early queer reliance on a narrative of quick, radical change are not hard to discern. Michel Foucault's influential work on "epistemes" and "the birth of the homosexual" suggested that radical change occurred in the past in dramatic fashion. Fundamental to Foucault's historiography was the exuberant philosophy of Friedrich Nietzsche, whose iconoclasm—"I am no man, I am dynamite" (Nietzsche 1969: 326)—provided an optimism and energy to queer theory that was highly motivational but also ripe for disillusionment. As I will explore in Chapter 1, Foucault and Nietzsche were and are enormously useful, but they are also highly problematic as sole theoretical touchstones.

Sexuality studies needs to be able to project a radically different future while also understanding the inevitably incremental nature of change—in identities, in institutions, and in categories of normality and abnormality. No matter how much Butler or Sedgwick you read (as the Deep Springers discovered), you cannot simply shatter your past sexuality and build a new one on the ruins of the old. Nor can we expect to shatter entrenched belief systems and expect a new configuration of sexual politics to emerge miraculously from its ruins. We have to be patient and persistent and yet find ways to retain our political enthusiasm. I argue that only by grappling with and even enjoying incrementalism can we avoid the trap of what threatens to be a deep and continuing "political depression," that in Lauren Berlant's words, follows upon the "draining" of energy when "for queers and feminists, the scene of sexual publicity becomes more defensive than oriented toward world building" (Berlant 2007: 433, 441). Queer activists and academics need to reinvest in the future-oriented work of world-building.

Other theoretical models can assist us here. Butler makes a surprising side comment in *Undoing Gender* when she reveals that after her senior year in college she traveled on a Fulbright grant to Germany to study with the philosopher Hans-Georg Gadamer (Butler 2004: 240). Even so, Gadamer's name never appears in any of Butler's works, except in a brief footnote in her first book, *Subjects of Desire*. This is an especially surprising omission in her 2005 book *Giving an Account of Oneself*, where she touches on many topics that Gadamer himself addresses: vulnerability, responsibility, and transformation. Gadamer, as I suggest below (and explore more expansively in my next chapter), is a particularly skillful reader of change, of agency, and of desires for instrumentality. I will argue throughout this book that sexuality studies can use Gadamer and his philosophical hermeneutics at this moment because we need a new reading strategy—a hermeneutics of sexuality—and a theoretical base that allows for a radically different future achieved incrementally through critical conversation and continuing political engagement.

To many, Gadamer will seem the farthest removed from radical critique of all the major twentieth-century philosophers. In his *magnum opus Truth and Method* from 1960, he argues for the power of both tradition and prejudice or (more accurately) pre-judgment in our world-views and processes of coming to understanding. Yet there is nothing static or cynicism-inducing about that pre-formation. Gadamer offers cultural critics a broad methodology for acknowledging and analyzing incremental change in the service of a radically different future. Tradition, as Gadamer uses the term, is the inevitable base matter of our perspectives and values. Prejudgments occur constantly in our daily lives as we negotiate our way through the complexity of incoming information and encounters with the partially known or unknown. These are phenomenological givens for Gadamer, and for many cultural critics who dismiss his work out of hand, that represents all they need to know to justify their stance toward him. "Gadamer!" someone once exclaimed when I opened a talk with a quotation from *Truth and Method,* "I can't believe you are quoting that dreary old thing!"

Some prejudgments do not stand up to sustained scrutiny, of course. Rather than celebrating or apologizing for tradition and prejudgment, Gadamer argues that both demand concerted, unending critical attachment, though any changes resulting from such engagement will occur only over long periods of time because of their continuing weight. Unlike theorists beholden to Nietzsche, Gadamer, trained by the neo-Kantians at the University of Marburg in the 1920s and 1930s, emphasizes slow processes of change rather than wholesale shatterings of belief systems or instrumental possibilities for self-alteration. This distinguishes him also from Giddens, the early Butler, and the entire cast of characters in *Bi-Ceps.* As I will explore in coming chapters, Gadamer's hermeneutics allows us to grapple with temporality and the embeddedness of our narrative-based identities, even as we retain discrete goals and radical, even utopian, visions of the future. Gadamer posits his own such vision: "The hermeneutical consciousness culminates not in methodological sureness of itself, but in the same readiness for experience that distinguishes the experienced man from the man captivated by dogma" (2003: 362). Unlike those philosophers and critics who posit full, final knowledge of both self and other as their "utopian ideal" (Gadamer 2003: 534), Gadamer's ideal is one of openness to change, of continuing explorations of the limitations of one's own perspectives and preconditionings, and, above all, of unending experimentation and enthusiastic interactions with interlocutors. Rather than citing Sedgwick, the Deep Springers might have looked to Gadamer to find theoretical justification for continuing their queer adventures, even if success was not immediately at hand.

For many of his recent feminist respondents, Gadamer's conversation-based, incrementalist approach holds considerable promise. Gadamerian theory recognizes the power of social conventions without assuming that they are unalterable and focuses on enthusiastic intellectual and political engagement as a key component of any process of alteration. Susan Hekman contends that Gadamer's critique of tradition offers feminism a singular opportunity to probe "how to effect change within the existing set of meanings that constitute society" (Hekman 2003: 184). While Foucault "claims that there are gaps and silences between discourses [and that] subjugated knowledges can rise to the surface, breaking the hegemony of established discourses of knowledge," he never tells us precisely how this can occur (Hekman 2003: 191). For Hekman, Gadamer fills in that blank: "Every experience, he claims, is a confrontation— it sets something new against something old. [...] The constant juxtaposition of tradition and new experiences, understood in the context of the historical situatedness of all understanding, provides Gadamer's hermeneutics with its critical possibility" (2003: 193). Of course, new situations and new information are often recuperated within old narratives or simply dismissed out of hand—indeed, that is why change is generally so slow—but the potential in the classroom, in political activism, and in responsible intellectualism generally is to bring the confrontation between old and new, tradition and revision, to a point of consciousness and overt expression. That is what *Reading Sexualities* will work to do in chapters examining queer activism, consumerism, literature, sex culture, and increasingly global circulation. Countering the depression, pessimism, and cynicism that seems to pervade much of queer studies today, my own contribution to the ongoing conversation in sexuality studies is relentlessly optimistic and enthusiastic.

Rather than positing "no future," the book you are now reading is all about the future, for as I will explore in my next chapter, Gadamer's overarching emphasis is on continuing conversation and investment in a future-oriented exchange of ideas and ideals. Thus he would never countenance the opting out that Edelman promotes. Instead, Gadamer would insist that even explicit projections of what constitutes a "better" future are neither normative nor prescriptive if we discuss them vigorously and use them provisionally, as critically adopted incitements to continued engagement. We in sexuality studies need such place-holding utopias— ones in which wide-ranging sexual diversity is valued highly, in which explorations of possible mutabilities in sexual desire (self-generated, theoretically generated, and simply temporally inevitable) are discussed energetically, in which the many ways that people engage in consensual erotic relationships are appreciated—and we need a mechanism to get us there: a missionary-like zeal for conversing among ourselves and with those who differ from us. We also need the intellectual quickness, flexibility, and tenacity to weather setbacks, shift tactics, and allow ourselves and our goals to alter in active dialogue with others. Marketplace acceptance and token media visibility, though useful, should never suffice as the telos of our work—they are simply a side benefit.

Our goals may be radical, but our political and pedagogical work is always done in slow negotiation with narratives that empower and constrain, with perspectives that shift slowly, with bodies that do not respond mechanically, and with a wide variety of competing voices and entrenched opinions. That enmeshment within the present and the past, even as we work toward an unknowable but still imaginable future, is hardly a reason to opt out. It is, instead, the simple phenomenological basis of life, even queer life, itself. Queer studies needs to acknowledge and work with that fact if it is going to *have* a future.

1 Sexual hermeneutics

A reading scene

I spent my adolescence in rural Alabama, surrounded by chicken farms and pine trees, after my father decided to flee the suburbs for small-town life in what he thought was a move to a safe, drug-free environment for his children to grow up in. Nothing could have been farther from the case since many of the bored teenagers in my junior high and high school were even more prone than suburban kids to taking the easy route of escape through indulging in angel dust, pills, and booze. In high school I tried alcohol and pot (which I didn't like at all), but years earlier I had already found my personal drug of choice in reading. I was addicted to science-fiction novels from age twelve onward, sitting for hours daily, devouring every sci-fi and fantasy book I could get my hands on. It was an intense high that I got as I sat in my bedroom and lost myself in narratives of time travel, intergalactic conflict, swords, and sorcery— anything that would take me out of the dreary sameness of rural life. Reading denaturalized my Alabama existence in thrilling and seductive ways—moving from the inside of my bedroom to the outside of the alternate worlds represented in the novels, and then from the inside of those books to the outside of my schoolwork and few friends, with both dynamics complicated even further by television, movies, and music. I quickly became adept at using those extra-local points of reference to begin to imagine possible futures for myself that were not limited by the Alabama state line (which few in my family had ever moved across) or the trade fields (heating and air-conditioning repair, plumbing) that my father presented me with as appropriate and stable career paths. I imagined that I wanted to be an astronomer ("You mean like one of those fortune-tellers in the newspaper?" my dad asked) or a diplomat ("Have you ever met one of them? No one around here does that") or a writer ("You don't ever plan on writing stuff that's not true, do you?"). My mother, every time I would announce that I had decided on a different career for myself, would hold her breath until I revealed it and then say, rather nervously, "Thank God, I was just sure you were going to say hairdresser this time."

Her fears were not unfounded. After all, "hairdresser" was one of the few commonly available career narratives offered to gender-non-conforming males. I was an effeminate little boy, prone to theatrics, and also prone to intense, barely concealed crushes on other little boys. My school and home were not exceptionally homophobic or violent places, but I knew well to keep my burgeoning queer desires to myself as much as I could. Sci-fi allowed me, early on, to imagine that there might be other ways of being and understanding that would validate (or at least accommodate) my desire for other boys, though certainly it offered no concretes. Sure, television occasionally offered up an acid-tongued, eye-rolling queer character (Paul Lynde, Charles Nelson Reilly) as an unap-pealing role model, but mostly I had to hope somewhat blindly that one day I would find my way out of dreary Alabama and into a place or space where I could kiss and cavort as I wished, one that I hoped would *not* be a beauty salon. I was often depressed—not about who I was or what I wanted, which I accepted without anguish from about age twelve on (coinciding with and no doubt connected to the beginnings of my sci-fi binge)—but rather about whether or not I would ever find an accept-ing and exciting social context. I remember when my brothers and I, in a particularly morbid conversation when I was thirteen or so, started pre-dicting how we each of us would eventually die (one predicted a car accident, another predicted a house fire). I announced that I would probably kill myself at a young age.

But I did not, and while I do not want to state that any one encounter or occurrence "saved my life," I do know that I started the journey from depressed young queer to fully self-assured proto-queer-rights activist when, at age fourteen, I happened upon and covertly read a copy of *The Happy Hooker* by Xaviera Hollander that my mother had secreted away in her bedroom nightstand. By sheer happenstance, Hollander provided a sex- and gay-positive voice that took me on a journey outside of the normal routines and values of early 1970s Alabama life. Glancing recently at the thirtieth-anniversary edition of the book (which was the first time since that early encounter that I re-read it) I can see why it had such a profound impact on me. Hollander recounts with unbounded enthusiasm her adolescent bisexual experiences and her later joy in hanging out at Dutch resorts with gay friends, as well as her admiration for their sex-positive attitudes. She also condemns explicitly the discrimina-tion against gays and lesbians that she witnesses in Johannesburg while living there briefly. Most famously, of course, she revels in her work as a hooker and madam in New York where she accommodates without moral judgment her clients' diverse desires, as long as they do not involve harm to others. My identity-political consciousness was raised significantly.

For my purposes in this and upcoming chapters I want to isolate two dynamics that the encounter above engendered within me. One mirrors that provided by science fiction. My reading was the occasion for an encounter between the circumscribed and oppressive micro-context of my life, with its few available narratives (air-conditioning repairman, plumber, or beautician), and a broader international and cosmopolitan worldview and more expansive set of narratives. By reading Hollander I was also able to read my life and my desires differently. Hollander further denaturalized the norms of my Alabama existence, and demonstrated that the world that I saw around me was only a small fragment of a diverse and exhilarating (both intellectually and sexually) world culture and conversation. As was the case with my encounter with science fiction, I was able to live a version of a hermeneutic circle, by which I partially glimpsed, partially imagined a broad and complex text and then returned to my small location in it with an adjusted and complicated understanding of it. Even more than with the fictional imaginings of sci-fi, Hollander's autobiography demonstrated to me that what I saw before me did not have to *be*, that one day, if I persevered, I too might travel the world, meet other people with desires like mine, find a fulfilling niche for myself, and even perhaps cross paths with Xaviera (whom I finally did meet a few years ago at a conference when I was able to thank her for the role she played in my life). *The Happy Hooker* allowed me to imagine a narrative for my own life that did not end in an Alabama beauty parlor and/or in suicide.

The other dynamic, connected intimately to the above, was political and utopian, though not simplistically so. By the time I read *The Happy Hooker,* I had read hundreds of novels, from Asimov to LeGuin to Zelazny. "Utopia" has long been a critically engaged concept in science fiction, and while characters existing in oppressive circumstances desperately need to imagine a "better" future for themselves, they rarely adopt visions of a perfect or conflict-free state (or if they do and achieve it, it turns out to be a dystopia of enforced homogeneity and totalitarianism). However, characters who resist effectively often depend on placeholders or provisional utopias that operate as motivational devices and tactically adopted blueprints for change. *The Happy Hooker* served that function for me in the realm of sexuality. The memoir certainly did not recount a problem-free existence of sexual liberation and unshackled pleasure-fulfillment. Hollander details acts of violence, blackmail, duplicitous treatment by loved ones, and unscrupulous business practices, ones that would not simply disappear if prostitution were legalized, as she advocates. Yet she certainly imagines a better future for herself if laws were altered. I too developed an identity politics, motivated partly by her vision of pleasant, relatively uninhibited sexual encounters and a supportive community of like-minded friends and partners. This projected, better future—a critically adopted, provisional utopia—was necessary for me to sustain a life in the midst of oppression, even as I knew that I was attaching myself to a projected life narrative that was only tentative and perhaps impossible. Provisionality is not a difficult meta-concept for a teenager to understand and embrace, though it is one we often forget or come to deride as we are called upon to make and defend decisions in our lives. Hollander well equipped me to begin strategizing about something concrete: how I could move to an urban area where I would find sympathetic companions and connect myself to a larger political movement that would work toward respect for sexual diversity. Hollander's world, as complicated and imperfect as it was, served as my placeholder, my provisional utopia.

Hermeneutic theories

In coming chapters I will explore how those two dynamics of change—a hermeneutics of expanded and complicated understanding and one of projected, provisional utopias—are keys to meeting the challenges of sexuality studies today. However, it is important to note initially that hermeneutic theory has never been referenced regularly in queer theory or other contemporary cultural theory, and there are several reasons for that omission. Part of the explanation may be timing. As Kathleen Wright has argued, Gadamer's *magnum opus, Truth and Method,* was published in 1960 but first translated into English in 1975, and was "eclipsed right from the start by the intensity of the discussion about the works of Michel Foucault and Jacques Derrida" (Wright 2003. 40). But beyond that unfortunate coincidence of translation dates, practitioners of what came to be called "cultural studies" were already suspicious of anything called "hermeneutics." Its most famous early theorist, Friedrich Schleiermacher (1768–1834), was a theologian whose interest in understanding texts was inextricably connected to his Christianity. Hermeneutics, in its long relationship to biblical exegesis, has always carried with it a vague association with religious conservatism, hardly a cause compatible with queer, feminist, and other identity political theorization. As we will see in examining Gadamer, even later hermeneutic theorists remain deeply interested in tradition, which seems, on the surface, wholly discordant with the iconoclastic principles of queer theory especially, devoted as it is to a radical engagement with the traditional reference systems delineating normality from abnormality.

Hermeneutics was tainted further with another of Schleiermacher's agendas: establishing authorial intent as the fundamental grounding for readers' understanding. For this reason, culturally and methodologically conservative critics in the mid- to late twentieth century (E. D. Hirsch, for example) occasionally still referenced Schleiermacher approvingly; he seems to offer an author-centered mode of interpretation that removes a text from questions of inherent ambiguity, linguistic and referential instability, and political tendentiousness. That too is inconsistent with the principles underlying cultural studies and identity political work. Cultural critics have long argued that "intent" provides no valid basis for interpretation, since reception and cultural usage is much more important in assessing the ways texts operate as cultural currency and conveyers of meaning. As we will see, Gadamer actually agrees wholly with that latter point.

Finally, hermeneutics became associated with a move to stabilize and systematize the process of interpretation, with its preeminent nineteenth century theorist, Wilhelm Dilthey (1833–1911), serving as a major advocate for making the humanities (*Geisteswissenschaften,* or human sciences) as rigorous as the natural sciences and as capable of rendering interpretive judgments with certainty. At the moment when Friedrich Nietzsche was calling for overturning systems of knowledge, Dilthey went in precisely the opposite direction, seeking to expand the systemization of knowledge bases. Dilthey's efforts were in vain, and later hermeneutic theory acknowledged that fact and repudiated the quest for systemization. Unfortunately, we today in cultural studies—anti-systemizers par excellence—seem to gravitate toward such a limited group of theorists and theoretical touchstones in constructing our arguments that we achieve in practice the systemization that Dilthey desired. The small corpus of widely cited theorists in queer studies—Foucault, Lacan, and, to a far lesser extent, Deleuze and Guattari—provide an even more static and predictable system to queer work today than one would find in most other fields.

In all of these ways and more, hermeneutics was anathema to much twentieth-century critical theory and certainly to the field of queer theory. As criticism generally moved toward an aggressive engagement with the political resonances of texts and the ways texts (and human expressions generally) are marked with traces of power relationships and a variety of unfinished social and psychological processes, hermeneutics seemed old-fashioned and politically retrograde. However, hermeneutics took turns after Dilthey that have barely registered among critics and theorists in Britain and the USA and that should make it of particular interest to those of us working in sexuality studies. Philosophical hermeneutics, the field originating in the work of Gadamer, departs significantly from the totalizing and methodologically conservative work of Schleiermacher and Dilthey. While both of those theorists were on a search for a static and definable "truth," Gadamer in *Truth and Method* foregrounds that word in a subversive way. There is no one, stable, enduring truth, according to Gadamer; there are methods of understanding that lead to our own localized versions of truth, ones that may be real to us, but that can never be captured with quasi-scientific precision (as Dilthey might have wished). In the words of Kurt Müller-Vollmer:

> Like his predecessors, Gadamer ascribes primary importance to the concept of understanding. But in contradistinction to Schleiermacher [and others] who conceived of understanding as a means of overcoming the historical distance between the interpreter and the historical phenomenon, Gadamer maintains the historical nature of understanding itself. Any interpretations of the past, whether they were performed by an historian, philosopher, linguist, or literary scholar, are as much a creature of the interpreter's own time and place as the phenomenon under investigation was of its own period in history.
>
> (Müller-Vollmer 2006: 38)

Gadamer embraces a form of historical relativism that disconnects a text or phenomenon from any essential "meaning," acknowledging instead that meanings are always socially constructed (though he never uses that precise phrasing). For Gadamer, that relativism does not forestall a search for "truth" in understanding, rather he sees that search as fundamental to human being in the world, even if "truth" as a static entity can never be pinned down.

Gadamer follows his mentor Martin Heidegger in starting from the principle that human beings are thrown into the world of phenomena and negotiate their everyday life and pursue their most cherished projects through processes of interpretation. In a dialogue with Paul Ricoeur, Gadamer states that Heidegger taught him "that interpretation doesn't *occur* as an activity in the course of life, but *is* the *form* of human life" (Ricoeur 1991a: 220). Behind that activity lies an injunction:

> I think Heidegger demonstrated that, behind the whole activity of human life, seeking its points of orientation as *In-der-Welt-Sein,* is

this mysterious openness to being which is inseparably connected with our finitude; an openness to questioning, an openness which lays the constant charge upon our human living to break through the illusions of our self-sufficiency.

(Ricoeur 1991a: 220)

The charge that he articulates there—to break from the debilitating and destructive belief in self-sufficiency—will resonate through the coming pages and chapters. Gadamer (in his refinement of Heidegger and in clear distinction to some current trends in queer theory) demands from us an intellectual humility and outward engagement that counters dogmatism, defeatism, and cynicism. From earlier hermeneutic theorists, Gadamer appropriates the model of a hermeneutic circle to theorize how such expanded and always renewed understanding is possible, though he also embraces the fact that this process is conducted always in language, with full recognition of the imperfect, changing, and inherently unstable nature of that medium.

Gadamer's revisions to earlier models are significant. Beginning in the early nineteenth century, the hermeneutic circle was a way of imagining how expanded or enhanced understanding might be achieved. In his musings on the field of historical research and historiography, the German thinker Wilhelm von Humboldt (1767–1835) suggested that historical occurrences could never be understood in isolation, that only through a consideration of a longer narrative of succession could the meaning of any one event be understood. Humboldt theorized the specific task of the historian as one of creating a narrative for readers that captured "truth." That stance (one might even say professional narrative for historians) held sway for generations, though Gadamer and most of us today would recognize immediately that historical narrative-writing is always biased and culturally limited. We write and narrate out of our own subject positions.

For Humboldt, that macro can be defined authoritatively by the historian, but we today, who admit and live with far deeper uncertainties, commonly work in more nuanced fashion by acknowledging that our understanding of the whole is also under constant revision as we revisit the micro or individual. Both are fluid but both are necessary for textual interpretation and for political action. As I read a novel, I place each sentence and action revealed therein into the context of my emerging understanding of the narrative. As I come to see myself as a politicized being, I place my individual experiences and needs into the context of an identity political group and that group into a broader ideological context of other social aggregates, distinct and overlapping, all with projected purposes that I imagine I understand (however imperfectly). In both instances, I am responsible for shifting my understanding and revising my perspective as new information and other voices present themselves. Hermeneutics has something to tell us about how we live as context-interpreting, intellectually flexible, political beings.

But Gadamer's revision of the idea of the hermeneutic circle is even more thorough than that. For Gadamer, our projective understanding of the whole must be subject to revision because it depends on prejudices and traditions that inhabit us and that we inhabit (and must come to modify). In Gadamer's words:

> The circle, then, is not formal in nature. It is neither subjective nor objective, but describes understanding as the interplay of the movement of tradition and the movement of the interpreter. The anticipation of meaning that governs our understanding of a text is not an act of subjectivity, but proceeds from the commonality that binds us to the tradition. But this commonality is constantly being formed in our relation to tradition. Tradition is not simply a permanent precondition; rather, we produce it ourselves inasmuch as we understand, participate in the evolution of tradition, and hence further determine it ourselves.
>
> (Gadamer 2003: 293)

This long quotation bears extended consideration because it indicates Gadamer's complicated relationship to the idea of any historical and contextual determination of the individual as well as the agency, and therefore *responsibility,* that the individual retains over and above any determination.

To understand the power of "tradition" it is first necessary to explore the Gadamerian notion of "prejudice." Though the English translation of *Truth and Method* consistently uses the word "prejudice" as the equivalent of the German *Vorurteil,* the better translation is "prejudgment." The word "prejudice," we might even say, prejudices us against Gadamer, who is neither an apologist for racial stereotyping nor for homophobia (though he has rightly been criticized for remaining silent on most identity political issues beyond his excoriations of antisemitism and the Nazi regime). Instead, he points to the fundamental fact that we move through our daily lives by using preexisting categories—traditions and place-holding assumptions—to process information and make sense of our world, and by projecting forward on the basis of provisional definitions and accepted versions of truth that we rarely attempt to test for their actual validity. If I see downed electrical wires on the sidewalk, I'll walk far around them rather than step on them, because I place those wires in the category of "danger" and prejudge them as a threat. If I know nothing about how refrigerators work, and my fridge suddenly emits smoke from the back and dies, I will not open its casing and attempt to repair it; I place refrigerator motor repair in the category of "specialized technical knowledge" and do not waste my time (and instead call someone listed categorically under "refrigerator repair" in the phone book, whom I prejudge as having the requisite training and ability). Those are among the innumerable mundane ways in which prejudgments are the base matter of our existence.

Yet that phenomenological process of hasty references often extends too far, which can lead to racial, gender, sexual, and innumerable other prejudices. These intellectually unsupportable and interpersonally harmful shortcuts are among those that the hermeneut should fixate upon, in Gadamer's opinion. Thus, one of the central questions in *Truth and Method* is "What distinguishes legitimate prejudices from the countless others which it is the undeniable task of critical reason to overcome?" (Gadamer 2003: 277). Gadamer's emphasis on critical attachment has also been that of identity politics in the past century. Common to the work that has been done in race theory, gender and feminist theory, queer theory, and Marxist/materialist theory is a common cause: demonstrating that prejudgment on the basis of the highlighted identity category is an illegitimate prejudice. Human being, we have commonly argued, is not reducible to the formulae of stereotypes.

Equally common to the supplest work done in identity politics is a second Gadamerian insight: that we are linguistically and culturally formed and that there is no pure space of reason untainted by residual errors in judgment and valuation. Gadamer writes, "there is undoubtedly no understanding that is free of all prejudices, however much the will of our knowledge must be directed toward escaping their thrall" (2003: 490). As we shall see, Gadamer repeatedly emphasizes this dynamic of maintaining an energetic, even idealistic, agenda, while he also reminds us of the forces that complicate our achievement of utopian goals and that moderate our expectations for swift and sweeping change. For Gadamer, the past is always with and within us, individually and collectively. In a famous passage from *Truth and Method,* he asserts:

> In fact history does not belong to us; we belong to it. Long before we understand ourselves through the process of self-examination, we understand ourselves in a self-evident way in the family, society, and state in which we live. The focus of subjectivity is a distorting mirror. The self-awareness of the individual is only a flickering in the closed circuits of historical life.
>
> (Gadamer 2003: 276)

That flickering does not predetermine our failure at interpretation, but he suggests that we must acknowledge it and remember our own capacity for error. Even the most radical among us live within history, its conditionings, and its discursive norms. We are bound to the past and present, even as we work toward the future.

And part of what we belong to is "tradition," another controversial term in the Gadamerian lexicon. He uses it to complicate any notion of swift and thorough change: "Even where life changes violently, as in ages of revolution, far more of the old is preserved in the supposed transformation of everything than anyone knows, and it combines with the new to create a new value" (Gadamer 2003: 281). He continues, "we are always situated within traditions, and this is no objectifying process— i.e., we do not conceive of what tradition says as something other, something alien. It is always part of us" (2003: 282). This dynamic is Gadamer's take on what some would term discursive preformation or acculturation, as he asserts: "Our historical consciousness is always filled with a variety of voices in which the echo of the past is heard" (2003: 284). While Gadamer is perhaps more sanguine about tradition than those of us working in identity politics are, he usefully checks our hubris in thinking that there is an "outside" to tradition that is accessible through instrumentally deployed reason or through iconoclastic fervor. As noted in the long quotation above, Gadamer fully allows that we participate in "tradition" and partially, collectively, "determine" its future. We have agency in Gadamer's opinion and because of that agency, responsibility also. But what Gadamer does is to confront us with our own imperfections, and slow down our expectations of change even in the context of our work toward a radically different future.

The question of how change occurs fascinates Gadamer. The two dynamics central to his reading of the change process are "fusion" and "conversation." Gadamer figures our position within a historical context and point of view as a "horizon," a spatial metaphor that indicates what is, and is not, visible to us given our sociocultural and temporal location. Our horizons shift, of course, as we move through time and through the various interactions that comprise even a single day's existence. All phenomena which impact us—whether as a face-to-face interaction with another person, or through reading, an encounter with visual media, or some other aesthetic experience—Gadamer describes as a meeting of "horizons" or points of view. These encounters happen across standpoint epistemologies—as in the case of two individuals discussing a political topic—and across time periods and historically situated belief systems—as when Gadamer reads a work by Plato or Aristotle. What occurs as two horizons meet and interact is a fusion of sorts. Ideally, when two individuals converse, each begins to shift or expand through the exchange process. Similarly, as I read, my worldview begins to shift or expand as I absorb the information and perspectives that I am encountering in print. Inevitably, we process from our own horizon, which means that in Gadamer's opinion, Schleiermacher's quest for original intent is an impossible one; we are bound by our horizons, even as those also always change over and in time. Gadamer concludes:

> In fact the horizon of the present is continually in the process of being formed because we are continually having to test all our prejudices. An important part of this testing occurs in encountering the past and in understanding the tradition from which we come. [...] Understanding is always the fusion of these horizons supposedly existing by themselves.
> (Gadamer 2003: 306)

How credible are Gadamer's claims here? "Fusion" does not imply replacement or any other form of necessarily radical alteration. Nor are the conditions under which horizons meet always ideal or even productive. Indeed, the modesty in his figuring of change makes this aspect of his philosophical hermeneutics useful, especially for those of us working in identity politics. Gadamer recognizes the power of social conventions without assuming that they are unalterable, and focuses on active engagement as a necessary component of any process of alteration. "Fusion" accommodates the minuscule changes that happen when we watch the nightly news and process new information, as well as the larger changes that might occur when we enter a mentoring relationship or read a revolutionary book and are confronted with startling new perspectives that we had never encountered before (as was the case for me the first time I read Hollander's book or, later, Foucault's works). The extent to which we are open to change depends, of course, on how we approach such encounters. Gadamer suggests that we have active (if always imperfect because tradition-influenced) choices to make regarding our openness to others and their points of view, while he recognizes also that we can never control how others might approach an encounter with us.

In the previously cited dialogue with his friend and fellow hermeneutic theorist, Paul Ricoeur, Gadamer writes,

> We can objectify ourselves; we can decipher the text of our own life, seeing it as a full series of symptoms of an illusion. And yet how can we make our way through this in a way that does justice to concrete life as an interpretive process? For me the pre-eminent model has been *dialogue*.
> (Ricoeur 1991a: 222)

Because Gadamer seeks to further significant change (especially in the weeding out of debilitating prejudices), he focuses on the conditions under which the most transformative forms of conversation can occur. He writes, "To be in a conversation [...] means to be beyond oneself, to think with the other, and to come back to oneself as if to another" (Gadamer 1989: 110). That is an idealistic statement, but Gadamer is deploying his own provisional utopia in theorizing the most productive forms of conversation that we should all attempt to nurture. His model of ideal, transformative dialogue consists "not in trying to discover the weakness of what is said, but in bringing out its real strength. It is not the art of arguing [...] but the art of thinking" (Gadamer 2003: 367). And for Gadamer, with his model of life itself as a process of epistemological fusion through conversation, the possibility for transformation is endless: "Each remark calls for another, even what is called the 'last word' does this, for in reality the last word does not exist" (Gadamer 2001: 59–60). As Fred Dallmayr notes, Gadamer's notion of dialogue signifies "not a sequence of soliloquies but an existential encounter involving mutual testing and risk-taking" (Dallmayr 1989: 84). Dialogue is a process of adventurous self-testing that Gadamer sees as fundamental to living life with honesty and passion. Indeed, he suggests throughout his autobiographical writings (especially in *Philosophical Apprenticeships* from 1985) that such humble, yet enthusiastic engagement is a particular responsibility of the professoriate and all others who consider themselves intellectuals.

What Gadamer foregrounds for us working in cultural studies and sexuality studies is the slow but relentless process of change and the openness and optimism that we should always bring to the process of furthering change. He provides us with a strong theoretical basis for the reparative hermeneutics that Eve Sedgwick called for in her work during the 1990s on potentially nonparanoid reading practices (Sedgwick 1997: 3). Similarly, he answers David Halperin's more recent call for "queer alternatives to the modern, scientific culture of the self and its psychological hermeneutics of the subject" (Halperin 2007: 8). Emphasizing that we are always as prone to error as our interlocutors, Gadamer asks us for generosity, flexibility, and humility, meeting Butler's request for "an acceptance on the limits of knowability in oneself and others" (Butler 2005: 63). Gadamer calls on us to speak out of self-admittedly limited subject positions, to *enjoy* the queer multiplicity of standpoint epistemologies, and to welcome potential critical responses as the foundation for all learning and enhanced understanding.

In discussing alternate possibilities for reading queerly, Sedgwick usefully (if only quickly) points to the work of Paul Ricoeur, who helps her call into question our reliance on a hermeneutics of suspicion and paranoia (Sedgwick 1997: 4–5). Ricoeur also assists us here in under-standing the change process by focusing intently on the narratives we embody and that metamorphose as we encounter other narratives, whe-ther represented by phenomena or embodied by other individuals: "the meaning of human action is also something that is *addressed* to an indefinite range of possible 'readers.' [...] All significant events and deeds are, in this way, opened up to this kind of practical interpretation through present *praxis*. Human action, too, is opened up to anybody who *can read*" (Ricoeur 1991b: 155). We are readers of each other, and we are characters in each other's narratives: "in our experience the life history of each of us is caught up in the histories of others. Whole sections of my life are part of the life histories of others—of my parents, my friends, my companions at work and in leisure" (Ricoeur 1992: 161). In textua-lizing our selves in that way, Ricoeur is not arguing that we are simply or statically scripted in our lives, or fall into the mistake identified by Henning Bech of psychoanalysts who ask for a "self narrative" that reveals truth, "a hidden and essential meaning" (Bech 1997: 144). Nowhere does he say that the "self *must* be narrated" and thereby write off the exis-tence of the unconscious (Butler 2005: 65). Ricoeur, like Gadamer, recognizes that there is no "truth" to identity, only methods leading to forms of imperfect understanding, achieved through the mundane inter-active process that he metaphorizes as a reading process. In the words of one recent commentator, "hermeneutics becomes a theory of the text, which takes texts as its starting point, but ultimately comes to see the world as textual, insofar as human existence is expressed through dis-course, and discourse is the invitation humans make to one another to be interpreted" (Simms 2003: 31). Our life narratives, imperfectly expressed and never clear even to ourselves, are entangled with those of many others, all inviting our active interpretation, and leading, through their critical juxtaposition and interaction, to a process of endless alteration and reevaluation. This process is what Butler has appropriately called our "chance of becoming human" through "our willingness to become undone in relation to others" (Butler 2005: 136), if we allow ourselves to challenge and be challenged. While my encounter with Hollander's life narrative certainly did not "make me" gay—I was well aware of my own bodily responses before I read her book—my processing of her narrative helped me change my perspective on my self and possible ways of being in a world beyond the boundaries of my rural locale. My horizon was shifted in new directions.

Ricoeur and Gadamer also shift the horizons of those of us working in queer theory, as their hermeneutics allows us to grapple with slow temporal processes even as we retain discrete goals and utopian or radical visions of the future. As I noted earlier, Gadamer references his own motivational ideal, one of attitude and awareness rather than sociopolitical prescription, that "readiness for experience that distinguishes the experienced man from the man captivated by dogma" (2003: 362).

Thus, throughout *Truth and Method,* he remains thoroughly skeptical of "the Enlightenment's faith in perfection, which thinks in terms of complete freedom from 'superstition' and the prejudices of the past" (Gadamer 2003: 273). "Belief in the perfectibility of reason" is as much a myth as the romantic nostalgia for some "paradisiacal primal state" (Gadamer 2003: 274). Philosophical hermeneutics embraces the imperfection of our understanding of self and other, and the never-ending quest for better understanding in spite of our common opacities. His commentary thus usefully augments an ongoing queer theoretical project that already rejects "that the scholarly ideal of dispassionate reflection, with reason as one's only guide, [because of its] refusal to recognize the multiple ways in which cultural and psychological factors influence what we think and write" (Turner 2000: 5). Such awareness should serve to render us all humble, though a question that will linger over upcoming chapters is the extent to which we actually practice what we preach.

Nietzsche, by way of Foucault

Praxis has always been an elusive goal in queer activism and academics, and while the theory base underlying early work in the field certainly provided a motivating energy in the quest for praxis, it is one that also warrants considerable complication. Butler, after working with Gadamer during her Fulbright in Germany, "returned to Yale as a graduate student and began to become politically active within the university, to read books by someone named Foucault, [and] to ask after the relation between philosophy and politics" (Butler 2004: 240). Foucault wholly supplanted Gadamer in Butler's burgeoning political consciousness, which dovetails with Wright's comment above that Gadamer's work was "eclipsed" generally by the intense interest in the work of Foucault and Derrida among intellectuals. Foucault was sexy, politically direct, and iconoclastic. Wright continues, "*Truth and Method* appeared overly conservative in contrast to Foucault's postmodern theory of the discontinuous nature and radical rupture from one *episteme* to another" (2003: 40). I too found reading Foucault a wonderfully dynamic and provocative experience; my graduate-school discovery of *Discipline and Punish* and *History of Sexuality* changed my perspective on texts, power, and the work of the cultural critic. Since I had earlier become engrossed in the work of Nietzsche, I was immediately taken with Foucault's work on the genealogy of seemingly natural yet thoroughly power-laden categories of social value and terms of identity. Genealogy was a tool that was easily manipulated and enormously helpful in the project that became known as queer theory, as it allowed cultural critics to trace the valence and historical specificity of concepts such as "perversion," "illness," and "homosexuality."

Yet explosive critique does not translate immediately or necessarily into explosive social change. The Nietzschean path, chosen by Butler and almost all of us two decades ago, is a very productive but also problematic one. Nietzsche, in the last section of *Beyond Good and Evil*, calls upon us to reject decisively the ease of social conformity and servility to common notions of the "good": "The noble type of man experiences *itself* as determining values; it does not need approval; it judges, 'what is harmful to me is harmful in itself'; it knows itself to be that which first accords honor to things; it is *value-creating*" (1966: 205). These may be highly motivational words for identity-political theorists—to invest oneself in denaturalizing "values" and critiquing the violence of common judgments—yet they are also ripe for disillusionment. As Wright noted above, much of Foucault's early work (*The Order of Things, The Archaeology of Knowledge*) imagined radical ruptures rather than incremental adjustments in processes of historical change. *The History of Sexuality, Volume 1* deploys similarly explosive language, the wide appeal of which led Michael Warner to assert that Foucault's theories were themselves explosive, constituting a "reinvigorating transformation" of sexuality studies (Warner 1993: viii). It is hardly surprising that Butler looked forward to ruins out of which new social relationships would surely emerge.

However, what such broad language does is mistake the possibility of a swift individual or even disciplinary reaction for a wholesale overturning of a social belief system or set of reference points. I have no doubt that Hollander raised my consciousness about sexual possibilities and alternate epistemologies; similarly, Foucault changed the way that I viewed power and resistance. But however much we might like to think of Foucault or Butler or ourselves (though our critical or political work) as "dynamite," to pick up on the Nietzschean phrase, the architecture of general social preconceptions, beliefs, and policies is not structurally fragile. As Alan Sinfield has noted, "One inference from antiessentialist theory *should be* that we cannot simply throw off our current constructions. We are consequences of our histories—those that have been forced upon us and those that we have made ourselves" (Sinfield 2004: 189, my italics). Unfortunately, our impatience can get the better of us.

Nietzschean theory may be critically useful and highly motivational but it grossly overestimates instrumental agency. It plays to our egos as ambitious activists and academics, but does not take into account the lingering and heavy force of social tradition. Thus, even as it enlivens the brilliant work of Gayle Rubin in her essay "Thinking Sex" from 1984 (which I will discuss in Chapter 5), it also leads her to the wildly inaccurate predication that reigning models of propriety and the scapegoating of nonconformists will have been wholly supplanted in "twenty years or so" (Rubin 1993: 7). Twenty years—specifically 2003—did see a US Supreme Court decision striking down state sodomy laws, but that was not a radical change, it was an incremental one. The voices of Rubin, Butler, and Foucault have operated as components of a broad social conversation that has also included the voices of Jerry Falwell, Pat Robertson, and even conservative gays and lesbians. All of those interlocutors have worked to slow down any hoped-for alterations in broad social attitudes toward diverse sexual practices. Horizons have fused and shifted; they have not exploded.

The slowness of the change process should not depress us or lead us now to opt out; its ongoing and relentless nature should invigorate us. Even changes in and with the word "queer" do not warrant pessimism. Halperin offers the following depressing assessment in *Saint Foucault* (1995), barely four years after the phrase "queer theory" was first used in the academy:

> "[Q]ueer theory" has [...] been transformed into an unproblematic, substantive designation for a determinate subfield of academic practice, respectable enough to appear in advertisements for academic jobs and in labels on the shelves of bookstores. Signifying little more than what used to be signified by "lesbian and gay studies," "queer theory" seems to have forfeited, in this process, much of its political utility. In any case, the more it verges on becoming a normative academic discipline, the less queer "queer theory" can plausibly claim to be.
>
> (Halperin 1995: 113)

That sense of disappointment (like de Lauretis's mentioned in my introduction) results from the dynamite model, one in which we wait expectantly for shattered ruins and an emergence of radical difference and then feel frustrated when nothing of the sort occurs. However, if we shift our reference points to think of "queer" as entering a conversation on sexuality and altering it gradually, even as it is used variously, then there is less need to feel betrayed or disappointed simply because "queer" becomes a widely circulated phrase whose meanings and uses have pro-liferated over time. It is Halperin, seemingly, who needs "queer" to sig-nify monolithically. "Queer" as a component of conversation can mean many things to many different interlocutors. Queer is dynamite, queer is category, queer is a work of densely written theory, queer is hairstyle and piercings, queer is an "eye for the straight guy," queer is a diverse body of theory, queer is, finally, what any one queer might say it is. That is a polyphony evincing a healthy and dynamic conversation. To cling to a "truth" about what "queer" is or must mean is to betray the very unsettledness that is queer theory's most provocative and useful innova-tion. There should be neither a fixed truth nor method to queer theory.

Life narrative

And this brings us to a final scene of "reading"—and readerly response—that will help me conclude this chapter. Though overly pessi-mistic at times, Halperin's *Saint Foucault* is nevertheless an insightful and revealing text. It demonstrates convincingly how central *The His-tory of Sexuality, Volume 1* was to the early queer activist and academic movements and then takes an interesting personal turn when Halperin discusses his own reading and writing life. He notes that he and several other critics were criticized roundly by philosopher Richard Mohr for an excessive regard for the work of Foucault; Mohr implies that Halperin in his book *One Hundred Years of Homosexuality* indulges in an "admiration for Foucault [that] has something irrational and excessive about it—something illiberal, idolatrous, fanatical, indiscriminate, hyperbolic, obscurantist, dogmatic, weak-minded, and superstitious" (Halperin 1995: 5). Halperin denies that was the case at the time but that in the five years since he wrote that book, "my admiration for Foucault and my identification with his discursive and political positioning have increased exponentially." He concludes: "So let me make it official. I may not have worshiped Foucault at the time I wrote *One Hundred Years of Homosexuality,* but I do worship him now. As far as I'm concerned, the guy was a fucking saint" (1995: 6). I have been led to similarly hyper-bolic assertions, citing Halperin's commentary in my book *Queer The-ories* and adding that "It is not at all an exaggeration to say that without Nietzsche there would have been no Foucault as we know him, and also without Foucault there would be no Donald E. Hall as I am constituted today. To Foucault I am indebted partially but importantly for my own queer 'self'" (Hall 2003: 67–8).

Foucault altered both of us, not through direct contact, but through a hermeneutic encounter. Halperin admits,

I know nothing about his life beyond what I've read in three recent biographies. [...] I never met Foucault myself. I never laid eyes on him. My relation to him is indirect and secondary: like my relation to virtually every other great writer, ancient or modern, that I have ever studied, it is entirely mediated, imaginary, and—why bother to deny it?—hagiographical.

(Halperin 1995: 6)

For Halperin, Foucault

grasped his total political situation as a gay intellectual and scholar better than anyone else has ever done. Moreover, Foucault's acute and constantly revised understanding of his own social location enabled him to devise some unsystematic but effective modes of resistance to the shifting discursive and institutional conditions which circumscribed his own practice. [It] was that ability to reflect critically on and to respond politically to the circumstances that both enabled and constrained his own activity that accounts for why Foucault's life—as much as or perhaps even more than his work—continues to serve as a compelling model for an entire generation of scholars, critics, and activists.

(Halperin 1995: 7)

Those long quotations capture a dynamic that is central to the present discussion. Halperin finds Foucault's theoretical implication of the ability to self-constitute and self-transform as intensely motivational, while the transformation in Halperin's own self occurred more slowly over time through the practice of reading about and reflecting on Foucault's life as a hermeneutic circle. A set of hermeneutic encounters led both to an awareness of a degree of agency in self-directed change and also was the mechanism for that change. The Deep Springers in my introduction did not find an erection mechanically at hand after reading Eve Sedgwick, yet there is clearly something about reading that can change one.

Gadamer describes it as a fusion of horizons. Ricoeur characterizes it as an encounter of narratives. The latter suggests that when we read we

seek in the text itself, on the one hand, the internal dynamic that governs the structuring of the work and, on the other hand, the power that the work possesses to project itself outside itself and to give birth to a world that would truly be the "thing" referred to by the text. This internal dynamic and external projection constitute what I call the work of the text. It is the task of hermeneutics to reconstruct this twofold work.

(Ricoeur 1991b: 17–18)

This is not simply an analytical process; it is also one in which we are "worked on" by the text, whether it is print, aural, or visual. As Ricoeur suggests in *Oneself as Another,* reading processes offer "a vast laboratory in which we experiment with estimations, evaluations, and judgments of approval and condemnation" (1992: 115). In our encounters with narratives, significant personal change can occur, as "imaginative variations on personal identity lead to a crisis of selfhood" through the denaturalization of the reader's preconception of how a life should or must be lived (Ricoeur 1992: 137). Every "fictive history" we encounter, he goes on to argue, "in confronting the diverse fates belonging to different protagonists, provide[s] [us with] models of interaction [...] clarified by the completion of narrative programs" (1992: 162). Reading alters one's horizon, to use the Gadamerian metaphor, and what is true for fictive histories is also true for every other encounter we have with the narratives of real, as well as imagined, human beings, in print or through any other means by which we make our selves, our perspectives, and our stories known to each other.

In reading and otherwise encountering the offered narratives of others (whether Hollander's, Halperin's, Gadamer's, our acquaintances', sexual partners', or life partners') we can assume a margin of leverage in reconstructing or renarrating our own lives. This is neither instrumental nor is it formulaic—we are neither scripted by that which we read or otherwise encounter nor are we allowed mechanical control simply to adopt or adapt others' scripts. But such encounters constitute the most significant mechanism by which we alter over time. When I read Hollander I was able to place my developing sense of a personal sexual narrative in conversation with that of another individual. I was taken "out of" myself and saw that self as differently positioned (and positionable) in a broader constellation of life styles and life choices. Halperin, in reading biographies of Foucault, was similarly affected. Neither Hollander nor Foucault serves as a model simply to be mimicked; even so, their narratives do serve as a source for what is commonly called personal and political consciousness-raising, a metatextual, hermeneutic experience. The sometimes chance-driven, sometimes purposeful and chosen activities, actions, and life components of others are the base matter from which our lives evolve, and to the extent that we have any agency in those lives, it derives from the extent to which we can reflect critically on the options presented to us. It is why I have never shied away from relating the "personal" in my "professional" publications and why I have treasured the all-too-infrequent autobiographical remarks of the writings of other academics, theorists, and activists, such as those offered by Halperin in the quotations above.

Yet we cannot forget that the critical capacity such narrative juxtapositions allow carries with it an equal measure of responsibility. Ricoeur's own purpose is not to establish precise formulae for moral behavior; he argues instead for "the primacy of ethics over morality— that is, of the aim over the norm" (1992: 171). That is a significant distinction, for he is burdening his own readers with the responsibility for discovering and exercising as much agency as possible and for acting always with ethical intent: "Let us define 'ethical intention' as *aiming at the 'good life' with and for others, in just institutions*" (Ricoeur 1992: 172, original italics). Those injunctions and their relationship to sexuality studies demand critical scrutiny always, but we can find in them a queer compatibility between Ricoeur's work and that of Michael Warner in such field-defining pronouncements as "Following Hannah Arendt, we might even say that queer politics opposes society itself" (Warner 1993: xxvii), meaning that following Arendt, queer politics must oppose "conformism, the assumption that men behave and do not act with respect to each other" (Warner 1993: xxvii). What Arendt, Warner, and Ricoeur collectively ask us to do is to "act" rather than simply behave, and to develop a critical and political consciousness concerning the modes by which proper "behavior" is defined and enforced. They ask us to adopt a praxis that maintains flexibility in our own positions and perspectives and that also values the voice and challenge of others as we seek the good life with and for them in just institutions.

Ricoeur, of course, leaves wholly and purposefully undefined what he means by "the good life," it not being his intent to tell people what to do. Instead, he asks that individuals develop a narrative distance on their own actions and especially interactions to enhance their ability to further individual happiness and institutions that protect the right of the individual to pursue whatever makes her or him happy within boundaries of respect for the other and the other's imperfections. Ricoeur's is as much a potentially radical queer ethics as Hollander's, Arendt's, and Warner's are. All four advance an ethics that derives from allowing individuals the ability to pursue happiness without interference except when impinging on the rights of others to pursue their own "life plans" (Ricoeur 1992: 157), while acknowledging the partial opacity of those very lives and plans. In Butler's words, it is an ethics "spawned by a certain willingness to acknowledge the limits of acknowledgement itself" (Butler 2005: 42).

Queer studies, to the extent that it retains its political edge, is bound up still with that old-fashioned process of consciousness-raising, a critical distanciation on one's own complicities and active choices—an analytically sharpened readerly response that should quicken our fervor but complicate our expectations of instrumentality, full or final understanding, and immediate payoffs. As my next chapter will examine, we are inundated with an increasing number and variety of queer texts, many structured by the easy and pacifying market-based narrative lines of queer consumerism and life "style." Yet even if we are told "queer" happiness can be purchased in the form of prepackaged vacations, sexy automobiles, and the fashionable clothing we must wear while vacationing and driving about, the question remains to what extent we are pursuing the "good life" with and for others in just institutions. The burgeoning queer media are proof only of the burgeoning need for queer critical reflection.

Warner refers to the "universalizing utopianism of queer theory" (1993: xxvi) as it seeks to embrace all who would work to resist regimes of the normal. While in the coming pages I will discuss such future-thinking as an engine driving queer studies and politics, here I simply want to affirm that Ricoeur's and Gadamer's works are also driven by the utopianism, antidogmatism and a "readiness for experience" that characterize queer theory at its most provocative and transformative. They offer us a theory of how to pursue the good life in just institutions, through conversation with each other, and by gaining the critical distance such conversations allow. At its most dynamic, queer theory is hermeneutic theory.

2 Desirably queer futures

Ecstasies

Among the many writers whom I regularly ask students to read in undergraduate queer-studies classes, I have several who are favorites because of the strong and diverse reactions they elicit. Early pieces by Judith Butler, as I indicated earlier, incite intense classroom discussions over agency and performative possibilities. Similarly, Gayle Rubin's "Thinking Sex" invariably causes a stir because of Rubin's searching analysis of the dynamics of moral panics in American culture (which students find useful a quarter century after the essay was first published), and because of her matter-of-fact discussion of all sexual diversity, including incestuous and intergenerational relationships. Reading Rubin always leads to heated and far-reaching classroom debates over what "is" and "is not," and what "should" and "should not" be, part of a queer theoretical agenda and a queer future of expanded sexual possibilities. The intellectual and personal investments that students bring to their positions and projections can lead to such agitated and engrossing exchanges that time often slips away from us in class; we forget the clock, our other materials assigned for the meeting, and our selves in their academic regularity. These, we might say, are ecstatic experiences, ones in which we are temporarily out of place, out of time, out of a corporeal self-awareness. Dialogue can do that to you; dialogue can do that for you.

Another of the writers whose work I often bring to class for reading and open debate speaks to this very state and some of the underlying needs it fulfills. In the excerpt I assign from Amber Hollibaugh's *My Dangerous Desires,* she writes, "Sex is the method I've used to search for wonder and awe. It is ecstasy I've craved and sought, nothing less. Sex is one of the few realms where my need for ecstasy was realizable, conceivable, resting on no resource save my own body and imagination" (Hollibaugh 2000: 263). We discuss that assertion at length, since for many of us there are a wide variety of nonsexual avenues for experiencing what might be called the ecstatic: dance, art, sports, even, as just mentioned, vigorous conversation. Yet Hollibaugh's own purpose is also much broader than a simple celebration of personal erotic exploration; she uses the concept of the ecstatic to critique the failures in imagination which she sees characterizing most sexual identity-political movements today. In her reading, today's "rights" movements have given up articulating a concrete vision of "sexual, economic and social justice;" instead, the "movement for gay legal rights [...] now parodies and duplicates a heterosexual middle-class/upper-class agenda based on recreating the rights of heterosexuals for gay people, with all the implicit and explicit pieces of class and race prejudice that go with it" (Hollibaugh 2000: 265). She notes that in responding to oppression solely through assimilationist strategies, "we gave up the fight for desire and sexual difference—as we gave up a more radical vision of the world we want to create" (Hollibaugh 2000: 266). The utility of articulating such a "radical vision" is indispensable for Hollibaugh, and her own vision is one which she proclaims clearly and unabashedly:

> We must, as a community, affirm desire. [...] The key to organizing around sexual issues, its incredible power, lies precisely here: erotic desire, whether couched as romantic or ferocious, is what will make most people risk everything. This is precisely because sexual fulfillment is where most people hope to find true ecstasy. And there is no human hope without the promise of ecstasy.
>
> (Hollibaugh 2000: 268–9)

Hollibaugh's commentary always ignites a lively classroom conversation. To what extent must we aggressively project forward—holding out hope for ecstatic or other radical transformation—in order to activate ourselves in the present? Students from the smallest towns and most difficult economic backgrounds are often the most eloquent on the topic of how necessary it is to imagine a radically different future in order to endure and then move beyond a life on the margins; they speak of their own process of politicization as one originating in an intense desire for a "better life," concretely, though variously, defined in terms of a fulfilling career, a life without fear of violence, a loving partner and set of supportive friends, access to healthcare, and so on. Their versions of radical transformation may not seem ecstatic in the sense that Hollibaugh affirms above but certainly encompass the hope of significant transformation of a current corporeal reality, and contain the promise of happiness through the achievement of (for them) elusive affective, political, and economic security goals. A few of their classmates, usually those from wealth and a comfortable suburban life, will roll their eyes, not understanding at first some of their colleagues' need to imagine a radical change to their current existences. Why imagine, or imagine working toward, big changes when one has almost everything one wants and when one can already project being able to buy what one desires and equates with fulfillment? A nice car, fashionable clothes, and summer vacations abroad are all within reach when one has a credit card with few limits. These clashes of perspective are eye-opening for all of us, as we discover that while material comfort has a role to play in most people's imagining of a "better life," it also proves to have a potential pacifying effect. An ecstasy of consumption can leave one corporeally sated and sluggish.

"What is the ecstatic?" we are led then to ask. Is it a moment of blissful forgetfulness? Or a loss of self-consciousness that persists for seconds, or minutes, or hours? A breakdown of language and paradigm that leads to a forever-changed perspective? Or a state of altered consciousness that, however profoundly experienced, dissipates inevitably under the weight of the returning world? My students' various answers to these questions can take us far and wide into their projections of what is and is not necessary for a better world, not just a better personal life, and what role sexuality plays for them in that world. We find that there is not one but many ecstasies: of the sexually responsive body, of sensual indulgence, of intellectual expansion and transformation, and of political fervor, among other possibilities. We lose ourselves in the fusions offered by conversations such as these, as we speak from selves that are at once resilient and always potentially metamorphic. Indeed, that tension between stasis and change is the Gadamerian substructure for all educational processes and for responsible intellectual activity more generally. While each ecstatic conversational experience may dissipate as we return to our normal routine, I know well that the incremental payoff of many such dialogic encounters can be powerful, even if experienced variously and unpredictably. I would never have become an educator if it were not for the promise of participating in students' continuing transformation through encounters in such broad flows of intellectual conversation. I would never have been such an avid reader if I did not experience those transformations firsthand. In fact, I would not be writing this book if I did not believe that my own contributions to an ongoing conversation might have the ability to transform the horizons of others.

Utopias

My perspective here is idealistic, no doubt, but such hope for the world-changing reflects the optimism that animates Hollibaugh's work, as well as that of other interlocutors whom I bring into the class conversation. Two statements that Michael Warner made in helping inaugurate the field of queer studies are ones to which we still attend. In his 1993 introduction to *Fear of a Queer Planet,* Warner states that "heteronormativity can be overcome only by actively imagining a necessarily and desirably queer world" (1993: xvi). Later, he expands on that thought in asserting that the

> universalizing utopianism of queer theory [...] has the effect of pointing out a wide field of normalization, rather than simple intolerance, as the site of violence. Its brilliance as a naming strategy lies in combining resistance on that broad social terrain with more specific resistance on the terrains of phobia and queer-bashing, on one hand, or of pleasure, on the other.
>
> (Warner 1993: xxvi)

Warner links acts of imagination—specifically, utopian thinking—with political efficacy and the ability to expose the workings of violence in everyday life. "Actively imagining" is the engine driving activism of a more hands-on sort, a point with which Paul Ricoeur concurs: "I believe, in fact, that there is a historic function of utopia in the social order. Only utopia can give to economic, social, and political action a human intention" (1974: 289). Hollibaugh, Warner, and Ricoeur remind us that it is difficult, if not impossible, to motivate ourselves and others if we do not allow ourselves to dream of a desired result to our efforts.

This may seem rather obvious, but "future thinking" of this sort has become the target of pointed critique even among those who term themselves queer. As previously discussed, Edelman excoriates such moves, arguing that our culture's obsession with the future embodies always a political conservatism that reproduces the same beliefs, ideologies, and social relationships, rather than produces the radical break with norms that queer theory and queer studies has called for since its inception. *No Future* argues that queers must insist that "we do not intend a new politics, a better society, a brighter tomorrow, since all of these fantasies reproduce the past, through displacement in the form of the future" (Edelman 2004: 31). Edelman concludes: what "is queerest about us, queerest within us, and queerest despite us is this willingness to insist intransitively—to insist that the future stops here" (2004: 31).

I respect the motivation behind such calls for a radical interrogation of the past and present, and certainly I am revolted by this country's continuing obsession with media-disseminated images of the "endangered child" (Edelman's biggest bugbear) which serve to further discrimination against queer would-be parents, to censor websites and ban queer-positive books from libraries, and to abet policies that target bars, bathhouses, and adult entertainment businesses. I too am thoroughly fed up with a politics of lying, manipulation, and scapegoating. However, my disgust at a political practice of fear-mongering and queer-bashing that frightens the public through predictions of a horrifically imagined queer future does not lead to a necessary abandonment of political engagement and queer intellectual investment in a *desirably* queer future. The latter does not follow necessarily or logically from the former. To repudiate any need to discuss, project, and contest a variety of possible futures is to retreat into silence and static self-referentiality. Solipsism and self-sufficiency should be the target of queer analysis, not its mode of being.

There is no transcendental, extra-discursive source of inspiration for the radical transformation of culture; there are only the concrete plans, projections, and negotiations that arise from our living, being, and interacting in language. I would have us then insist intransitively that the future *starts with us*—collectively and by way of our individual articulations, choices, and narrative fusions and collisions. In Gadamer's oft-quoted phrasing: "Being that can be understood is language" (2003: 474), to which I would add that what we do not express or project concretely (even if imperfectly and out of substantial self-opacity), we never have to defend, revise, or come to understand any of the limitations of. As is obvious throughout this book and clear from my choice of theory base, my ecstasy is a language-based ecstasy, as much as I respect Hollibaugh's desire for transcendence through sex alone. Mine is an ecstasy of shattering the illusion of self-sufficiency and escaping the trap (and tedium) of self-referentiality by engaging enthusiastically with others, with a view toward an ever-widening understanding of the idiosyncrasies of the self-generated perspective. Rather than retreat into silence about what we desire for ourselves and our queer community/communities, I want us to move in precisely the opposite direction, to embrace a radical imaginative and conversational practice that acknowledges the force of the past (or tradition, as Gadamer would term it) but that resists any determination by it, and then projects forward in detailed and imaginative ways. Through conversation we can queer and re-queer each other.

Acknowledging the past always raises the specter of nostalgia, but that is neither my own impulse nor was it Gadamer's. Even as I find it useful to reference Michael Warner's and Judith Butler's work from the early 1990s (responsible pedagogy and research always demand an acknowledgment of preceding voices leading to the current conversation), I would never suggest that we try to reclaim the urgency of the early queer activist movement when an entire generation of gay men was dying of

AIDS as the Government and public looked on with indifference. No one would wish to return to such a horrible era, even if possible, and certainly nostalgia for past political successes or modes of organizing does not serve as any motivation for work today. An obsession with the past—whether idealized, aestheticized, or even accurately remembered—is as much a distraction from the hard work facing us now as is a passive hope that somehow it all work out for the better without any active investment of energy or imagination or political fervor.

Yet nostalgia is not our only or greatest distraction. In embracing future thinking, I want to disrupt also our preoccupation with the easy, seductive indulgences of present consumerisms. "Trust" that it will all "work out" without a precise program or set of goals can go hand in hand with, and will too often countenance, an overreliance on the media and marketplace as an indicator of significant change and as a force that is sufficient in fostering such change. It is a mindset articulated by a wealthy, self-identifying "queer" student I once had who often rolled his eyes at classmates who mentioned political activism and whose utopian vision consisted solely of "a sexy car, a cute boyfriend, and a big, fat paycheck." His was an exaggerated version of the desire for base-level economic security articulated by some of his working-class colleagues, one that mirrored uncritically a media image of happiness defined by acquisition alone.

That mindset of happiness-inducing consumerism is promulgated by the glossy gay and lesbian magazines that are available now on newsstands across the country, even in Alabama and West Virginia. In a recent issue of *Out* (August 2007), the only concrete interest in the future I could find was that expressed in an article previewing the fall television line-up. Aaron Hicklin's brief "Editor's Letter" in the issue did comment on the "good news" of a changing political climate (as evidenced by a vote in the Massachusetts legislature against a proposed anti-gay marriage amendment), but he attributes it largely to the force of media representations, to *"Will & Grace, Brokeback Mountain,* and the launch of Logo." He concludes that "Old-fashioned activism might have played a big part in the Massachusetts vote, but I'm willing to bet that in a roundabout way [Jon] Stewart, [Stephen] Colbert—and, yes, even [Adam] Sandler—played their part too" (Hicklin 2007: 16). While he devotes several column inches to those heterosexual celebrities who poke fun at queer-phobia, he offers not a word beyond the above to "old-fashioned" activism. Television and print media, and the innumerable advertisements in the magazine which he edits, appear to carry the weight of social change that "old-fashioned activism" *might* still contribute to (though obviously he is skeptical). There is no future imagined by *Out* beyond ever-expanding entertainment, clothing, and fragrance options. The only ecstasy is that provided by consumption.

Admittedly, some good does come from marketplace and media visibility, and I would not want to discount wholly the positive effect even of consumerism in and on processes of social change. Katherine Sender writes cogently about the complexity of such effects in *Business, Not Politics: The Making of the Gay Market;* among her points is that a queer-positive

> ad from AT&T is not evidence that the battle for gay rights is won, but nor does it herald the end of a gay fighting spirit. Gay readers engage with advertising thoughtfully and with multiple commitments and desires, even as it is impossible to know what the range of those commitments and desires may be.
>
> (Sender 2004: 241)

However, even she readily admits that the marketplace is not fundamentally progressive. She concludes, "it is inherently frustrating to put faith in the consumer sphere as the route to acceptance; for all its pleasures, to hope for political gains in the increasingly desperate attempts of corporate America to court gays and lesbians is to put trust in a fickle creature" (2004: 242). Fickle, it is. If we ever reach a point where the unborn can be tested for likely future sexual preference, media and the marketplace will jump on that predictive capability even if it colludes completely with queer-hating eugenics. Markets are opportunistic, and when queer-fearmongering stories sell newspapers and lead to increased hits on news websites (and therefore increased ad revenue), the engine of competitive capitalism is just as happy run on the fuel of homophobia and sex panic as it is on the energy of queer consumerism. I'm as happy as anyone to see boys holding hands with boys, and girls with girls, on television (and hope that queer youth in rural America are less self-hating because of it), but occupying a recognizable market niche is hardly my idea of ecstasy.

Consumption can be pleasurable and addictive (I've blown my budget before on CDs and books), but it is not socially transformative in any ethically responsible, much less queer or radical, way. Alexandra Chasin notes that "consumption has been held out as a route to political and social enfranchisement" (2000: 101) but has worked in limited ways to that end most often by way of enfranchisement into a public sphere of exacerbated insecurity. Is it intrinsically *better* to hate ourselves for being as fat, wrinkled, and unfashionable as heterosexuals than it is to hate ourselves for being homosexual, transgendered, or bisexual?

Perhaps now we can at least take comfort in the fact that, advertising tells us, we can spend our way to happiness through weight-loss programs, skin-care products, and expensive clothing purchases, and can just be as happy as all the heterosexuals spending their way into bankruptcy because of their insecurities. That is progress of a very limited sort.

Yet much is lost thereby. Sender reminds us that the

> myth of the ideal gay consumer as affluent, educated, apolitical, and tasteful [...] obscures the ongoing fact of antigay discrimination in laws, employment, and cultural life [as it] encourages conformity to normative sexual, family, and social standards, and assumes that the checkout line and the voting booth, but not the street, are the appropriate places for political activism.
>
> (Sender 2004: 239)

Lisa Duggan has termed this the "*new homonormativity* [...] a privatized, depoliticized gay culture anchored in domesticity and consumption" (2003: 50), or what activist Mattilda Bernstein Sycamore has more pointedly derided as "a vapid, consume-or-die, only-whites-need-apply version of gay identity" (2008: 4). The range of observations above complement a set of similar points made by Ricoeur almost forty years earlier, when he noted that

> the consumer society towards which we are advancing in the course of this century has a profoundly ambiguous significance. On the one hand, it undoubtedly represents progress—a better living for the masses who have access to basic goods. [...] But at the same time, this universal civilization exercises on the creative nucleus of each of the historical groups an eroding action and a subtle destruction.
>
> (Ricoeur 1974: 291)

Gay-friendly shops and salespeople are all well and good, but surely the queer community needs to imagine and work toward achieving something more and better than what Gap, Pottery Barn, and Target will provide us at an 18–24 percent interest rate.

We need a new queer utopianism that is passionately articulated, energetically debated, and highly motivational. And there is a small but growing body of theoretical work that points in that direction. José Muñoz affirms that "Queerness is always on the horizon. Indeed, for queerness to have any value whatsoever, it must be considered visible only on the horizon" (2006: 825). He states that we in queer activism and academic work must look aggressively to a radically different future, saying that "hope is spawned of a critical investment in utopia that is nothing like naïve but, instead, profoundly resistant to the stultifying temporal logic of a broken-down present" (2006: 825–6). This means imagining beyond the components of a desirable lifestyle and the obsessions of the day and thinking critically and creatively about where we want to be, how we want to be, in a queer, queered, future. Muñoz calls on queer theorists "to summon a refunctioned notion of utopia in the service of a subaltern politics" (2002: 93), to fuse thereby utopian thinking and social critique. Frankly, I am less confident than he is that the "anticipatory illumination" of "art" and "culture" can "cut through fragmenting darkness and allow us to see the politically enabling whole" or that such "illumination will provide us with access to a world that should be, that could be, that will be" (Muñoz 2002: 108). Yet if we consider any glimpses of an imagined and only provisional "whole" (whether provided by art, culture, or vigorous interpersonal exchange) as ones that allow us to revisit hermeneutically the present with a critical consciousness, and that a revised understanding of the present in turn works also on the very future we are imagining, then we may be on firmer theoretical ground. That circularity is the Gadamerian notion of hermeneutic provisionality and process of enhanced understanding that I am exploring throughout this book.

As Jill Dolan, reminds us, "the word *utopia* means, literally, 'no place,'" one that she refuses to pin "down to prescription" (2005: 7). However, utopian projections are necessarily concrete—even if no-placed—and the question lingers how such projections avoid the trap of prescription. Dolan's vision of such provisional thinking is one which allows "fleeting contact with a utopia not stabilized by its own finished perfection, not coercive in its contained, self-reliant, self-determined system, but a utopia always in process, always only partially grasped, as it disappears before us around the corners of narrative and social experience" (2005: 6). I suggest that this partiality and provisionality is most productively realized and reiterated through the medium of conversational exchange. The Gadamerian process of concrete conversational contribution and earnest eagerness for others' rebuttals destabilizes any supposition of "finished perfection." The more explicitly we can articulate our visions, the more likely we will learn from others about the limitations of those projections. Dolan cites the work of Angelika Bammer to suggest that we "need to reconceptualize the utopian in historical, *this*-worldly terms, as a process that involves human agency" (2005: 6). That sense of agency, however tentatively imagined, drives political activism, cultural critical production, and other forms of applied intellectual and political work. That sense of critically and self-consciously imagined agency must offer itself as an alternative to the facile forms of agency allowed by the queer media and marketplace.

My contention is that utopian thinking can be strategically deployed without realizing *No Future's* prediction of prescription if we offer our individual visualizations and projections of an "ideal" or simply "better" world as self-admittedly no-placed and provisional, as ones that we are personally and intellectually invested in as conversational and motivational placeholders. This follows the Gadamerian process by which we enter a conversation with strongly held beliefs but ones that we advance *so that they may be revised* in dialogue with others. That means we have to love the learning process more than the sound of our voices and sanctity of our own perspectives, a humility which is also key to the utopian thinking that Gadamer explores in *The Idea of the Good in Platonic-Aristotelian Philosophy*. In writing about the extremity of the utopian political prescriptions articulated by Plato in *The Republic*, Gadamer writes:

> One thing is clear in any event: This ideal state cannot be actualized. [...] But what is the whole point of Plato's invention? That we see its absurdity? Is it meant to highlight the impossibility of the ideal? Are we supposed to read this political utopia only negatively and be convinced by it only of the irreconcilability of theoretical and civic life? If so, a great expenditure of intelligence and wit has been wasted. [...] On the contrary. Surely one must read the whole book as one grand dialectical myth.
>
> (Gadamer 1986: 70)

For Gadamer,

> reading dialectically does not mean taking the opposite of what is said, to be the true belief. [It] means relating these utopian demands in each instance to their opposite, in order to find, somewhere in between, what is really meant—that is, in order to recognize what the circumstances are, and how they could be made better.
>
> (Gadamer 1986: 71)

Calling this the "game of utopianism," Gadamer asserts that it is one in which "foresight and insight are attainable within certain limits" (1986: 73). While I would dissent from Gadamer's strictly dialectical model of utopian imaginings necessarily confronting their exact polar opposite, clearly dialogically engaged utopianism should return to what Gadamer calls "'real' historical life" in a way that generates the critical consciousness that constitutes "insight." This is a conversational process that might happen within an individual who projects in utopian fashion and then returns to the practicalities of the present, or much more productively, it is a process that happens among individuals who articulate their projections and then engage with each other on the perspectives generated and any possible "in betweens" or refinements that might be discoverable or negotiable. Ricoeur points to this utopian dialogics when he speaks of a "back-and-forth movement," "the intermediary zone of exchange between the undetermined character of guiding ideals and the determinate nature of practices" (1992: 157–8). Gadamer and Ricoeur point us to a utopianism that is provisionally advanced, critically engaged, and always conversant with possible practices.

Ricoeur is one of the most eloquent spokespersons on behalf of the political and critical use of utopian thinking: "From this 'no place' an exterior glance is cast on our reality, which suddenly looks strange, nothing more being taken for granted. The field of the possible is now open beyond that of the actual; it is a field, therefore, for alternative ways of living" (1986: 16). He finds useful a wide variety of imaginative wanderings: "some utopias legitimate all kinds of sexual community, while others endorse monasticism. With regard to consumption, some utopias advocate asceticism, while others promote a more sumptuous lifestyle" (1986: 16). But their overarching utility is clear for Ricoeur:

> This development of new, alternative perspectives defines utopia's most basic function. May we not say then that imagination itself—through its utopian function—has a *constitutive* role in helping us *rethink* the nature of our social life? Is not utopia—this leap outside—the way in which we radically rethink what is family, what is consumption, what is authority, what is religion, and so on? Does not the fantasy of an alternative society and its exteriorization of "nowhere" work as one of the most formidable contestations of what is? [...] The nowhere puts the cultural system at a distance; we see our cultural system from the outside precisely thanks to this nowhere.
>
> (Ricoeur 1986: 16–17)

Utopianism is thereby indispensable for social critique and social change. While Ricoeur in *Lectures on Ideology and Utopia* examines the many ways in which ideology structures utopia and is replicated within all utopias, he (unlike Edelman) never loses faith in the ability of the imagination to perform a critique of ideology through such future-oriented thinking. Following analysis of Karl Mannheim, Saint Simon, and others, he concludes, "At a time when everything is blocked by systems which have failed but which cannot be beaten—this is my pessimistic appreciation of our time—utopia is our resource. It may be an escape, but it is also the arm of critique" (Ricoeur 1986: 300). When concretely articulated and collectively debated, utopian-based critiques represent "queer" at its greatest potential—a verb both transitive and transformative. Utopianism is queer theory's most powerful resource.

A bright future

Such powerful and practical utopianism is hardly the domain of academic philosophers alone. In fact, given some queer commentators' scorn for the concretely projective, pop culture can be a much more vibrant realm and mechanism for provisionality and utopian thinking. Just as consumerism is, itself, neither purely good nor purely evil, so too is popular culture far from homogenous, and often it is complex enough to be both dependent upon the dynamics of consumer culture for its circulation at the same time it is invested admirably in a critique of those forces which shackle us to the most traditional forms of interpersonal relationship and social interaction. I mentioned Xaviera Hollander's and Amber Hollibaugh's work earlier as constituting laudable forms of such public intellectualism, and turn here to another widely read activist/ writer working recently along the same lines: the bestselling author, editor, and lecturer Susie Bright. Her *Full Exposure* is well worth bringing into our conversation for she shares many of the concerns expressed here, as she decries "our culture's [...] endless emphasis on material gain and status" (Bright 1999: 96) and offers instead a concrete, future-oriented perspective on radical sexual transformation.

Bright's title derives from her emphasis on conversation and narrative exchange as essential for such transformation. While her language may be more consistently accessible than Ricoeur's or Gadamer's, her implicit theory base is nevertheless strikingly "hermeneutic." Bright opens with the following observation:

> There is no such thing as a person without an erotic story. I don't mean a tall tale or a punch line or a story about the one who got away. I'm talking about a personal erotic identity, what you might call a sexual philosophy. [...] Take a look at your own erotic story, and you'll see that it's a motion picture of everything about you that is creative: the risks you'd be willing to take, the weightless depth of your imagination, your attraction to the truth, and the things that would make you go blind. That's a story all right. It doesn't matter

whether we tell it to a crowd of thousands, whisper it to our lover, or merely confess it to ourselves. The power is in owning it.

(Bright 1999: 1)

While an academic/theorist might find much to critique above—the hyperbole of the "everything about you that is creative" and the instrumentality of the "power [of] owning it"—Bright's basic assumptions are not far afield from that of Gadamerian and Ricoeurian hermeneutics, namely, that identity is based in narrative and malleable through time and by way of interpersonal exchanges. "Every time I've been changed by reading a book," she writes, "it was because the authors asked me the right questions" (1999: 3). What she asks of her readers is what Gadamer asks of all readers/interlocutors: that they allow the hermeneutic experience to disrupt the sanctity of supposed full self-knowledge and self-sufficiency. Bright "exposes" as fully as possible her own sexual philosophy to readers and expects them to do the same in conversation with others. Through that act of exposure in "endless discussions" she notes that we are offered the opportunity to confront "our personal prejudices" (1999: 82), much as Gadamer suggests.

Bright's emphasis on radical, far-ranging conversation is meant to further a process of "sexual liberation, whether it's given that name or not" (1999: 76), and it is tempting to let a discredited phrase such as "liberation" distract us here, but it should not. A provisional telos such as "liberation" can be motivational and even indispensable if we adopt it with self-awareness. Such critically adopted teloi are acts of politically motivated, narrative generation—useful, even if wildly imaginative and always open to revision. In her conclusion, Bright cites de Tocqueville: "In revolution, as in a novel, the most difficult part to invent is the end" (1999: 156). "Liberation" is a fictional invention—a utopian one to be sure—but such endings are necessary for narrative progression, even if that process of change is neither linear nor unproblematic. The important thing, rather, is to be brave enough to articulate a vision and then welcome an energetic discussion of it in the service of continuing, critically engaged change.

Bright cites Wittgenstein's observation that "Nothing really exists except examples" (1999: 5) to illustrate her overall point that the only leverage one has over one's own opinions and incorporations is that provided by narrative exchange. To that end, she offers an extended "erotic manifesto" (1999: 2), imagining a utopian world in which the concept of sexual orientation will "bust open [... so] it will be come clear to everyone that we've only made these stupid categories so that some people could fancy themselves superior to others" (1999: 16). In her conclusion, she then urges her readers to "roll out your own erotic manifesto" (1999: 156), one that she recommends sharing widely with others. As these manifestos/utopias are brought into contact with each other, she reminds us to "take inspiration from everyone and instruction from no one" (1999: 157). Narratives are not formulae for instrumental adoption; they demand critical attachment even as their multiplicity allows for interesting, idiosyncratic combinations. The upshot of this should be that our narratives are complicated beyond simple description: "Next time someone asks you what you 'are,' sexually, tell them that nouns will not do. [...] Labels, every one of them, should be saved strictly for protest signs and sandwich boards" (Bright 1999: 158–9). In making that last comment, she allows that labels carry political weight and are necessary to adopt in a struggle for identity-based rights; however, our critical adoption of those labels must be as self-aware as our critical adoption of our own provisional utopias. "Full exposure" means being willing to generate narrative in full view of others and also to let others challenge those narratives and their underlying assumptions.

The result of such queer, queered, and queering narrative exchange should be a renewed sense of personal, and just as important, political vibrancy. Bright speaks of this as "the love of a vision" (1999: 125) that serves to bind a movement together even as it "crumbles" and must be rebuilt at times. Her macro-utopia is one of radical conversational practice in the service of wide-ranging political transformation. She summons an "army of lovers" committed to the revolution of sexual self-revelation (1999: 143). While her emphasis on conversational openness and transformation through dialogic exchange may sound banal to some, it challenges many of the practices of academic professionalism, as well as personal self-promotion and self-protection. As I will explore in my next chapter, such openness is scorned by some homosexuals.

What we have to learn

Following Bright and Gadamer, I would have us invest enthusiastically in a dialogue on possible queer utopias that offers concrete visions of radically different futures, that seeks commonalities among individual projects and projections, but that also allows for and even welcomes profound differences. And in doing so, we have to be honest with ourselves that such projections will not cause the world to change overnight or lead to the overthrow of all norms and traditions. Gadamer reminds us that the fantasy of a "dissolution of every obligation to restraint," what he terms "an anarchistic utopia," is guided by a "hermeneutically false consciousness" (2006: 291). That false consciousness, when exposed as such through its underlying program's inevitable lack of realization, is bound to result in disappointment, despair, or even worse. In Peter Sloterdijk's analysis, "Cynicism is *enlightened false consciousness.* [...] With the passing of defiant hopes, the listlessness of egoisms pervades. In the new cynicism, a detached negativity comes through that scarcely allows itself any hope, at most a little irony and pity" (1987: 5–6). When hope for the future fades, irony offers a hollow sense of empowerment. It is an attitude without a defined politics and without an explicit program that must stand up to critical scrutiny and defend itself in dialogue with others. In its arch performance of superior knowing, irony seeks and admits no rejoinder, barricading itself against any challenge that might reveal its limitations. Like Paul Lynde performing his caustic shtick on *Hollywood Squares* in the 1970s, irony reads the other without allowing the other any legitimacy of response. Butlerian parody may have been a problematic action plan, but irony is a dead end.

We have too much to talk about as activists and sexual radicals to let irony suffice. Let's take our cue from Bright and push ourselves to generate utopian projections that we share energetically ... the bolder, the better. Expanded access to healthcare and an end to discriminatory practices are very modest common denominators of political purpose that we can get trapped in and by. They constitute the half of the political equation that is practical and immediate (and that I certainly devote considerable political energies to achieving), but without any forward projection to the utopian. In direct contrast to Edelman, both Hollibaugh and Bright worry that *without* a radical utopianism—a concrete imaginative practice—we inevitably replicate the known and capitulate to the most conservative forces. Thus Lisa Duggan points out that

> many of the dominant national lesbian and gay civil rights organizations have become the lobbying, legal, and public relations firms for an increasingly narrow gay, moneyed elite. Consequently, the push for gay marriage and military service has replaced the array of political, cultural, and economic issues that galvanized the national groups as they first emerged from a progressive social movement context several decades earlier.
>
> (Duggan 2003: 45)

In a void of radical projections, assimilation rushes in with its well-defined program. When imagination is squelched and would-be iconoclasts simply roll their eyes, those who do speak determine the future. The moneyed elite may be blameworthy, but silent bystanders have no reason to self-congratulate.

Queers must speak out concretely and enthusiastically. I (like Holli-baugh, Sycamore, and others) am disgusted that so many lesbians and gays, and all of our national organizations, obsess over the formalities of marriage, a bankrupt heterosexual institution that as often as not leads to wrenching divorces. Given the grotesque extravagance of many mar-riage ceremonies and equally grotesque demands for extravagant gifts from registries at Macy's and Saks, I suspect that much of the collective obsession with weddings is simply consumer mania overwriting more imaginative alternatives. So here is my first concrete articulation of a personal, provisional utopia: a world without the musty formalities, syrupy sentimentalisms, and gross consumerisms of institutionalized marriage. I agree wholly with Jacques Derrida, who when asked about "gay marriage" in his last interview said, "If I were a legislator, I would propose simply getting rid of the word and concept of 'marriage' in our civil and secular code" (2007: 43), though he fully admits that such thinking is "utopic" (2007: 44). I echo Derrida's queer conversation starter: let's not legalize gay marriage, let's abolish heterosexual mar-riage. That would make the world a much more interesting place.

But even if I don't get much political traction for that provisional utopia, the "sanctity" of marriage (gay, straight, or transgendered) is hardly the only topic that we as a queer community regularly refuse to address in radical, imaginative fashion. We need to have difficult, but intellec-tually invigorating, conversations on a host of other issues that are all avoided by assimilationists and for which irony or silence serves no use:

- Monogamy: I want to live in a world where we can do with our bodies what we wish, even as we maintain rich emotional ties and nurturing relationships—in pairs, groups, and networks of choice. We need to discuss more deliberately and precisely how those rela-tionships can be developed and maintained in the face of over-whelming cultural pressure to conform to the dyadic structure of two people in a monogamous pairing, too often controlled by the weighty and destructive myth of a "soulmate." I don't have a soul, much less a mated one.

- Age of sexual consent: This is the most taboo topic in American society generally and certainly in talking about homosexual relation-ships. Fear has silenced us completely on the topic. Even if you don't agree with Gayle Rubin that all forms of intergenerational erotic activity should be countenanced—unequal power relationships of many and various sorts make that a dangerous path to tread—it is still worth discussing at length at what point individuals should have the right to do with their bodies what they wish: twenty-one, eighteen, sixteen, fourteen, twelve? Wrangling about the pros and cons of varying possibilities along such a continuum can lead to heated and useful discussions as we confront how consent is given and whether intergenerational relationships can ever arise in nonabusive fashion. Remembering my own experience of sexual self-awareness, I vote for sixteen as a reasonable, nationally consistent age of consent and majority (for sex, drinking, legal accountability, and so on) instead of the USA's current mishmash of contradictory laws and policies. I believe we are increasingly infantilizing young adults, but feel free to disagree.

• The complexities of any concept of universal "queer rights": The question of age of consent confronts us immediately with that of cultural difference. Since fourteen and fifteen are ages of consent in some European countries, what does this tell us about "universal" sexual rights? If sexual contact between an eighteen-year-old and a fourteen-year-old constitutes sexual abuse in the USA, are people somehow intrinsically different in Estonia, Hungary, or Iceland, where it does not? Should we seek to impose a single conception of queer rights globally and thereby erase all local notions of what sexual activities are proscribed and prescribed? Do global queer rights include the right to universally available strap-on dildos and shirtless circuit parties from Harrisburg, Pa., to Riyadh, Saudi Arabia, to Maputo, Mozambique? Is that neo-colonialism or are there universal human "rights" that transcend more local "rights" to cultural difference and definitions of modesty? I will have much more to say on this topic in Chapter 4.

These and other controversial issues are precisely the ones that deserve the most radical activist attention and active academic discussion. In tackling them we are compelled to ask ourselves what we imagine as components of a desirably queer world and how we can get there. Such issues take us far and wide in conversation when I bring them up for discussion in queer-studies classes, and what happens in queer classrooms must happen in the queer community more generally. I urge us all to think of the most vexed issues involving sexual identity-political rights and responsibilities and talk about them concretely, argue about them, write about them, and get each other all aggravated and agitated. We should not opt out of conversation; rather, we should channel the energy of conversation into a radical queer activism for the twenty-first century. Disagreement and difference are signs of intellectual health and political vibrancy; a queer world in which all queers believe the same thing, maintain a polite silence about their differences, or simply roll their eyes at each other or at assimilationists is not a desirably queer world. That is not my idea of a utopia; that is hell.

For this conversational process to succeed, we must embrace, indeed love, a state of healthy disagreement and wrangling with difference. We must shift from an ideal of tacitly arrived at or carefully (often artificially) constructed consensus of the Habermasian sort and instead celebrate and value "dissensus" of the Lyotardian and Gadamerian sort, in which the value of difference and the value of the process of talking over, through, and about differences is held as one of the highest social goods. Ewa Ziarek terms this an "ethos of becoming" (rather than one of "arriving" or "agreeing" as Habermas would advocate). She sees dissensus as an engine driving "the creation of new modes of being, eroticism, social relations, and, ultimately, new models of democracy" (Ziarek 2001: 219). J. Hillis Miller sums up his thoughts on such possibilities in similar fashion:

> For Lyotard the social other—for example, the racial, class, gendered, or political other—is truly other. My values cannot by any means be reconciled with the values of someone who is "other" in one of these ways, nor can they be subsumed at some higher level that will encompass them both. Only a democracy based on dissensus and on some idea of radical heterogeneity in different persons and groups within a single polity could recognize and protect this radical otherness. "It seems to me," says Lyotard, "that the only consensus we ought to be worrying about is one that would encourage this heterogeneity or 'dissensus.'"
>
> (Miller 1999: 161)

Gadamer complements this notion with his desire for energetic and destabilizing conversation. Fusions and commonalities will emerge, inevitably, as we discuss our perspectives and projections with personal passion and intellectual energy; however, we also must approach the conversational process knowing that we have something to learn from and about others, about their standpoint epistemologies, and about our own limitations. Those differences are ones to celebrate because they are a mechanism for self-disruption and even the experience of an ecstatic loss of selfhood. All of us involved in the queer conversation participate thereby in a potentially ecstatic pedagogical process—as both educators and learners.

Indeed, we even have something to learn from our angriest and most objectionable interlocutors. The anti-queers have their radical vision of a theocratic state with a Big Brother-like government enforcing a rigid heterosexual agenda and dictating precisely what we can do with our bodies. That is their utopia, one that gets people to the voting booths and protest rallies and makes them feel that they are contributing to a holy cause. I want that passion for us—not one centered solely on material consumption or solipsistic self-promotion but one of intellectual, political, and conversational generation—as we devote ourselves to creating a desirably queer future.

And I use those words "passion" and "desirable" because what I am advocating here is built on and around our desires and our loves, much as Hollibaugh celebrates and as Muñoz too calls for in his hope for "better relations within the social that include better sex and more pleasure" (Muñoz 2007: 460). Unless we are narcissists, difference is the well-spring of our love and ability to love. "Homo"-sexuality is actually a misnomer for what many of us feel and enact through our desires—it is not "desire for the same" that we feel but rather love of the profound differences that exist even when the contours of two people's genitalia may be similar. In a very real sense, then, queer sexuality is actually "heterosexuality," though not in a way that most heterosexuals would accept. I love and desire my partner because he is different from me; we are a heterogeneous, mixed-race, queerly non-soulmated couple with very different personalities, ways of interacting with the world, and interests. If we recognize all sexuality as "hetero," one version of a desirably queer future is one in which that queerness—that hetero-ness—in all of its manifestations can thrive. Those who attempt to prescribe a narrow version of what we call "hetero-normativity" are the least "hetero" of all—they are homo-genizers, the anti-heteros, the ones who would not see my love of difference as "homo" enough. Perhaps that's our next big fight—for queer folk to reclaim the "hetero" for ourselves and brand the homo-haters the true homo-sexuals.

This emphasis on love and desire brings us around again to our investments in the future. Thomas Alexander in a provocative essay entitled "Eros and Understanding" suggests that Gadamer's conception of all successful relationships depends on future-thinking. This is true, Alexander notes, in pedagogical relationship, where the loss of the self is necessary for student and teacher as both focus on the ways individuals become part of and help alter communities (1997: 336). And it is also true of individuals in political relationship: "The task of hermeneutics, which is that of the constant recovery and transformation of the community, can do more than merely hope for future good: it must actively realize it" (Alexander 1997: 342). Finally, it is true of individuals in loving interpersonal relationship. In Alexander's paraphrase of Gadamer, "while I cannot go beyond finitude, I can go beyond *my* finitude in the moment when I become genuinely open to another. [...] Through our capacity to love, we achieve a finite transcendence" (1997: 340). He concludes, "The future opens up [...] as the possibility of the continuity of meaning through openness to the other" (1997: 340). This finite transcendence is one form of the ecstatic that I find convincingly theorized. The potential for such transcendence links teaching, activism, energetic conversation, and loving interpersonal relationship.

In all of those, we have to love our differences and our ability to learn from others more than we love our own personal agendas and solipsistic visions. We have the responsibility to risk ourselves—and the sanctity of our worldviews—in speaking out. That outward engagement runs counter to the inwardness of much recent academic and queer theoretical performance, even as that performance is beginning to attract some high-profile critics. David Eng quotes a statement he heard Gayle Rubin make at a conference a few years ago where she called explicitly for more "gay humility" in our academic conversational practices. He adds that "Rubin's call for 'gay humility' serves as heuristic device for a return to what a desirably queer world might look like" (Eng 2005: 15). I echo Eng's and Rubin's perspectives here. An offering of a concrete projection and provisional utopia, if it advanced as such and if accompanied by a request for rejoinder, is not only usefully ego-disrupting but possibly world-changing.

My desirably queer world is one in which our diverse loves, our political passions, our sexualities, our genders, and our senses of selfhood are all held up to vigorous communal discussion and loving appreciation even in the process of dissent and critical engagement. Our common fight for the right to our diverse selfhoods and sexualities must be the source of our political passions. While consumer culture has recognized the LGBTQ market as a consumer niche, it has also worked to "homo"-genize that market. We are all treated as if we were narcissists willing to do anything to look like the impossibly beautiful (because airbrushed) gym-bodied models who populate *Out, Curve, Instinct* and similar magazines. Our love for our own differences in sizes and colors and shapes and points of view is the antidote not only for the shame that the queer-haters try to foist on us but also the shame that the queer-exploiting market tries to create and manipulate in us.

That is a future that I will work toward with passion, and however others' visions of the future may differ, we should come together in loving but vigorous discussion to chart out strategies to move us slowly but steadily out of the morass of token media validation and assimilation into the monotonous, deadening, normal life that drove many of our parents into divorce and depression and life crisis. We can never break neatly from traditions, ideologies, and cultural norms, but we can critique them, move them, move from them. As Ricoeur notes, "We cannot

get out of the circle of ideology and utopia," but in discussing energetically and judging practically what can be done with specific utopian
agendas, critical judgment "may help us understand how the circle can
become a spiral" (1986: 314). That spiral depends on an energy greater
than the static circularity of consumerism and political cynicism. Our
collectively generated and hotly debated utopias and activisms should
take us to very different places.

3 Transcending the self

In the remaining chapters of this book, I will address some of the thornier issues raised in my previous discussion. What constitutes a Gadamerian "openness" to others? How would that openness manifest in concrete practices as our lives intersect in erotic and nonerotic ways? What agency do we possess in seeking or welcoming opportunities for encounters that could lead to shifts in our epistemological moorings? Finally, does a hermeneutics of sexuality depend on forms of objectification—interpersonal or intercultural—that are uni-directional and necessarily destructive? In considering these and related questions, I will move in and out of fictional texts, memories, memoirs, and political movements. As we will see, the question of how movement itself affects or does not affect us is central to any discussion of change—personal, political, and/or erotic.

The genre of travel writing contends with some of the same questions in ways that initially seem far removed from the field of sexuality studies but that prove to bear significantly on the discussion at hand. In a posthumously published essay appearing in *The New Yorker* (and collected later in the book *Travels with Herodotus*), the Polish journalist Ryszard Kapuściński reflects on his first trip abroad, his expectations concerning and then the reality of the experience. He writes of the anticipation:

> I wondered what one might experience upon crossing the border. What would one feel? What would one think? Would it be a moment of great emotion, agitation, tension? What was it like, on the other side? It would, of course, be [...] different. But what did "different" mean? What did the other side look like? Did it resemble anything I knew? Was it inconceivable, unimaginable? [...] This was only about crossing the border—it made no difference which one, because what was important was not the destination but the mystical and transcendent act.
>
> (Kapuściński 2007: 58)

Kapuściński ponders how epistemological change occurs and, specifically, how it relates to decisive acts. Might border crossing, by way of travel or a similarly sought-after encounter with otherness, produce a "mystical" experience? What happens, or can happen, to us when we decide to journey to a foreign place or previously unknown space? In moving through our heterogeneous world do we ever transcend anything?

The short answer to that last question—as casual and qualified as it must be—is "maybe" and "sort of," as Kapuściński himself discovers. On that first trip abroad, in the late 1950s, he was sent as a newspaper reporter to India, one of the few non-Soviet Bloc nations that wanted to establish ties to Poland, and was asked to file stories that, in his editor's words, "were supposed to bring that distant land closer" (Kapuściński 2007: 58). Even in that charge—as commonplace as it sounds—there is the underlying supposition that the potentially mystical and transcendent could prove to be or be made to be recognizable, accessible, and epistemologically proximate. Clearly, any encounter with difference, whether through travel, reading, aesthetic experience, or other means, is always potentially a vehicle for rendering the "foreign" knowable and managable through the imposition of knowledge and categories that precede the encounter. "They are just like you and me" is one possible response to difference that means that I don't have to question my pre-suppositions or limitations (beyond perhaps the prejudice that "they" are so different as to be inhuman or contemptible). Certainly many package vacations work to that end, turning the encounter with the sites and faces on the other side of the tour bus window into a safe historical narrative, one recounted by a guide and then cushioned by the cookie-cutter hotel rooms and bland buffet meals that bracket each day's experience.

However, that did not turn out to be the case for Kapuściński, and for a variety of reasons. Certainly his ignorance played a major role in the profound impact of the experience, for he was as wholly unprepared as he was eager for the trip. His editor sent him to India on a moment's notice, he spoke little English and no Hindi, he had no contacts in India, had no time to educate himself about cultural differences there or about the mundane difficulties of living in a "foreign" place, and had no actual plans for what to do after he arrived. After traveling for two days, he disembarked from an airplane in the middle of the night in New Delhi and felt a profound epistemological and phenomenological shock. Kapuściński writes, "I was left alone and had no idea what to do. The airport building was small and deserted [...] It stood all by itself, cloaked in night, and I had no idea what lay beyond it. [...] Nothing like this had ever happened to me before" (2007: 61). Indeed, the extremity of his situation makes it a particularly useful case for examining the question of how "openness" relates to personal agency. "Cast into deep water," he writes, "I didn't want to drown" (Kapuściński 2007: 62). On the surface we might say that Kapuściński reacts quickly in the service of simple self-preservation (with the only alternatives being psychosis, catatonia, or perhaps suicide). However, he also had significant attitudinal choices to make. After the initial shock wears off and with the help of some kind New Delhians (who use gestures to communicate with him and basically lead him by the hand), he commits to doing the hard work of opening himself up to interactions with the foreign "others" whom he encounters. He dedicates himself first to learning how to converse with them: "I realized that only language would save me" (Kapuściński 2007: 62). Granted, his rhetoric remains that of self-preservation, but rather than barricading himself in one safe place, he plunges also into the continually unsettling experience of seeing as much of the diverse Indian subcontinent as possible: "I could only move forward. I decided to travel" (Kapuściński 2007: 62). He studies Indian languages, cultures, and religions, questions others and listens attentively to their stories.

"Transcendent and mystical" may be problematic ways of describing the experience; however, it was certainly a life-altering one for him. We might even say that something was shattered forever—his illusion of self-sufficiency—though much remained in the form of personal history/ traditions and prior conditioning. He was not a new person but a different one by way of travel and his decisions regarding it. By the time he returns to Poland, he has complicated thoroughly and irrevocably his perception of the world and of himself, even if he feels like a failure because the trip undermined his easy sense of mastery. He concludes:

India was my first encounter with otherness, the discovery of a new world. It was at the same time a great lesson in humility. I returned from that journey embarrassed by my own ignorance. [...] I tried to forget India, which signified to me my failure, its enormousness and diversity, its poverty and riches, its incomprehensibility had crushed, stunned, and finally defeated me. [...] But of course I remembered India. The more bitter the cold of the Polish winter, the more readily I thought of hot Kerala; the quicker darkness fell, the more vividly images of Kashmir's dazzling sunrises resurfaced. The world was no longer uniformly cold and snowy but had multiplied, become variegated: it was simultaneously cold and hot, snowy white but also green and blooming.

(Kapuściński 2007: 65)

That is not "transcendence" in the sense of a move to an outside that allows a comprehensive or divine perspective on his existence, nor is it "mystical" in the sense of being related to something supernatural or otherworldly. Nonetheless, it does demonstrate the process of fusion that Gadamer advances as the best of what can happen in an "open" encounter. In choosing to learn from others (about their language, religion, perspectives) Kapuściński also learns through his encounter with otherness about the limitations of his own worldview; he "transcends," you might say, the illusion of full self-knowledge and self-sufficiency. He is taught—or more accurately, allows himself to be taught—the lesson that Gadamer asks of all potentially "cultivated" individuals: that of their own ignorance.

Travel, if it is ethically and intellectually responsible and responsive, *should* be epistemologically unsettling, should teach one profound lessons, even if one tries to prepare oneself more carefully than Kapuściński did. Certainly I have learned much through acts of dislocation. In 1984, after finishing an MA at the University of Illinois, I joined the Peace Corps and accepted a teaching assignment at the National University of Rwanda. I prepared as diligently as any comparative-literature graduate student could. I read everything I could find about Rwandan history and geography, studied French, and pored over narratives detailing other people's Peace Corps experiences, imaginatively trying on those stories as ones that might prove to be my own. Trying my best to control what would turn out to be an uncontrollable encounter with difference, I was just as clueless as my Polish predecessor.

In early summer, I was sent to do advanced language training at a school in Bukavu, Zaire (now the Democratic Republic of Congo). I boarded an airplane in Jackson, Miss., where I had stayed a couple of weeks with my parents, changed planes at JFK, and again at Charles de Gaulle in Paris, and then began the long journey down the west coast of Africa on a flight that stopped in Senegal, Ivory Coast, and Cameroon, before finally arriving in Kinshasa, Zaire. I had not slept in two days and then discovered at the airport that all my luggage, which I had packed with teaching materials and essentials for a two-year stay, had been lost or stolen. I was finally put on a bus at about 10 p.m. to go sleep for a few hours at a small hotel before catching another early flight the next day for Bukavu, still half a continent away. As I sat on that bus from the airport while it drove through shanty towns on the outskirts of Kinshasa—seemingly endless expanses of mud and cinder-block huts with no electricity but bathed in light from fires burning in large steel barrels and filled with people talking and going about their business and living their lives in a way that was unlike anything I had encountered before—I distinctly remember thinking to myself: "This feels like death." "This feels like death." Not because I thought someone was going to kill me but because sleep-deprived, baggageless, and surrounded by languages and images and smells and other totally "foreign" sensations, I "felt" that epistemological, phenomenological shock that Kapuściński calls "mystical," even though I had probably prepared myself as well as I could have. My illusion of self-sufficiency was shattered. I "felt" that I was in an abyss of incapacity, ignorance, and vulnerability. And, frankly, that was a useful and productive thing for a middle-class Southern white boy with a newly minted master's degree to experience.

I emphasize "felt" in what I just related because of course there was no radical change in or mystical shattering of my core selfhood. For one thing, I was working for the US Peace Corps, which had arranged for the bus, paid for the hotel, guaranteed (to the extent they could) my safety, provided me with language training over the next three months in Bukavu, and then with a place to live and a monthly pay check for the next two years in Butare, Rwanda. And even beyond the material consistency of my life, I was still largely my old "self," my accumulated knowledge base, my core beliefs, my likes and dislikes, all of which constituted my horizon (as Gadamer would describe it), even if that horizon shifted, expanded, uncomfortably encountered, and responded to—fused with— the differing horizons, values, and beliefs of many others over the next two years. I left the Peace Corps experience significantly changed but not through a mystical process, and, again, only in a broad way could one call it a transcendental one. It was much more banal and incremental than that—I talked to my colleagues in my imperfect French and Kinyarwanda, felt often like a failure, asked questions, and tried to listen attentively to the many differing opinions of those whom I encountered (Rwandan, Zairois, Burundian, Kenyan, Belgian, French, Canadian, Cameroonian). I heard about intense material hardships, about simmering tribal and racial tensions (exploding just a few years later in the genocide of the early 1990s), about varying professional aspirations and personal fears, and about community-based projects and intellectual pursuits that were previously unimaginable to me given my US-based training. Needless to say, I learned some valuable lessons about my own stupidity, ethno-centrism, and privilege.

I also learned that I could change, survive, and even thrive through and despite that shock that I just mentioned. Sara Ahmed, a British queer theorist of Pakistani family background, writes in *Queer Phenomenology:*

> What I remember, what takes my breath away, are not so much the giddy experiences of moving and the disorientation of being out of

place, but the ways we have [finally] of settling; that is, of inhabiting spaces that, in the first instance, are unfamiliar but that we can imagine—sometimes with fear, other times with desire—might come to feel like home. Such becoming is not inevitable.

(Ahmed 2006: 10)

Her last assessment certainly rings true. The process of settling implies a process of change, growth, and epistemological complication that follow significantly from the choices that one makes regarding the encounter— choices of inquiry, or defensiveness, or reactionary judgment, or safety through distance, or, perhaps, openness.

Such choices attending geographical and epistemological dislocations are much more common than one might initially think. Not all of us join Peace Corps or are sent abroad on journalistic assignments. Yet while I have been speaking here of travel experiences that may seem specific to the relatively privileged classes, the same processes regarding movement and the challenge of responding to difference follow upon any significant physical displacement. Poor, rural West Virginia students who receive scholarships and are the first in their family to go to college arrive in the small city of Morgantown to attend university and are sometimes overwhelmed by its complexity and diversity. How they will process difference and allow it to enrich their perspectives (or cause them to flee back to the homogeneity of their rural county) results not only from a myriad of personal, psychological, and familial factors but also from ongoing decisions that they make. While I am not denying that some individuals are better equipped than others to handle such challenges—shyness, paralyzing self-consciousness, and the after-effects of trauma are among the many elements that may lie wholly outside of an individual's control—I will continually return to the margin of choice that we do possess. In that boundary area—lying between determinism and full instrumentality—we can locate our ethical responsibility. Every person encountering difference—as a leisure traveler, freshman at college, conscripted soldier, even refugee—has some margin of choice to make regarding the processing of the encounter with otherness. To think otherwise would be to deny that person her or his base-level humanity in our process of analysis.

Gadamer too addresses that potential within all of us, asserting that we only live ethically by interacting responsibly. We are offered innumerable opportunities in our lives wherein we can *choose* to put our "prejudices" or presuppositions at risk by actively seeking out others with whom to share ideas, test our notions of reality, and come, through an exchange of viewpoints, to some, even marginal, understanding of our own mistakes and misapprehensions. If we see this as the opportunity to allow ourselves to be queered by others and for others to be queered by us, then a Gadamerian queer theory has something profound to say about living a life of intellectual and ethical responsibility. Risk-taking, especially in the risking of our core beliefs and sense of self-satisfaction, demands a conscious decision to prioritize the queerly interpersonal over the selfish and self-serving. A queer philosophical hermeneutics suggests that we can only move from solipsism to responsible social, intellectual, and ethical life by embracing our need for and responsibility to others, and for finding ways of engaging others in self-disrupting dialogue, providing us with at least a glimpse of a "macro" beyond the self with which to understand better or differently the "micro" of our own perspectives. However, a queer Gadamerian hermeneutics also reminds us that unlike when we are reading a print text, when we are dealing with the text of our fellow intellectuals, travelers, and inhabitants of the planet, we have the opportunity and responsibility to ask questions, solicit responses, request clarifications, and explore energetically that "outside" that may lead us to alter the "inside" of our own beliefs and localized interests. Gadamer urges us to talk to others, to listen to them, to learn from their differing perspectives, and then to return to our selves with a complicated and expanded vision. We would make a terrible mistake if we think we can "read" others' motives and perspectives from a distance, without engaging the human beings behind the "object" that we believe we are interpreting. Textualization of the sort I am broadly discussing here, by way of hermeneutic theory, always carries with it the risk of a unilateral and dehumanizing objectification if it is not based in the openness and self-questioning that is fundamental to Gadamerian theory.

In the remainder of this chapter, I will examine two fictional texts that explore such potential movements of the self through encounters with others: James Baldwin's *Giovanni's Room* and Leslie Feinberg's *Stone Butch Blues*. While both investigate the external forces trapping the self within the self, I will read the extent to which they also hold the self responsible for its interactions with others and how, through those interactions, the self can choose to be at once transformable and transformative. While Feinberg is the writer most explicitly probing a "stoniness" that appears counter to the openness that Gadamer calls for, it is Baldwin who most pointedly warns us of the terrible consequences of living within a stony butchness that repudiates interpersonal responsiveness and responsibility. In the next chapter, I will examine more fully how one's responsibilities are even heavier when one encounters others whose languages, cultures, and material positions in the world are especially precarious. Yet even in examining Baldwin's novel, we will see that class and cultural privilege are always potentially destructive forces.

Butch and blue

Baldwin's critique of the deadly effects of self-absorption is a central thematic component of *Giovanni's Room*. Its young American narrator, David, flees upper-middle-class suburbia of the mid-1950s, yet in doing so he seeks through travel an escape from responsibility and responsible communication rather than opportunities for new forms of self-awareness through encounters with others: "I had decided to allow no room in the universe for something which shamed and frightened me. I succeeded very well—by not looking at the universe, by not looking at myself, by remaining, in effect, in constant motion" (Baldwin 2000: 20). As suggested earlier, movement and ensuing encounters with difference do not lead necessarily to radical or even significant epistemological change; travel can be safe, numbing, or even destructive depending on how one approaches the experience. The lingering question, then, is the extent to which we are able to choose our approach.

The novel supports a queer Gadamerian perspective on agency and responsibility by suggesting, even from its early pages, that one cannot gain a perspective on a "self" that one has pointedly decided to ignore. After an unexpected night of "great thirsty heat, and trembling, and tenderness" with his best friend Joey, David reacts in a self-protective but ethically irresponsible fashion: "I made my decision" (Baldwin 2000: 8–9). He chooses to repudiate his homosexual desires, a choice that he makes internally and silently: "I did not tell him my decision [and] he did not know how to protest or insist. [...] The manner of my leave-taking had begun a constriction, which neither of us knew how to arrest" (Baldwin 2000: 9). In denying his queer self, disavowing his desires, and refusing even to converse with Joey—from whom he would have continued to learn about that queer self—David retreats from growth-inducing vulnerability and honest interpersonal exchange into a violent masculinity: "I picked up with a rougher, older crowd and was very nasty to Joey" (Baldwin 2000: 10).

Granted, the novel does not deny the context in which David makes his destructive choices. He "was ashamed. [...] A cavern opened in my mind, black, full of rumor, suggestions, of half-heard, half-forgotten, half-understood stories, full of dirty words" (Baldwin 2000: 9). And in having David's father nickname him "Butch," the novel clearly critiques an entire system of exaggerated and oppressive American gender norms that infiltrate David's perception of self and other. David must contend with powerful narratives of normal masculine behavior holding sway during a notoriously homophobic era, the 1950s. However, the novel also follows Gadamer and Ricoeur in suggesting that reigning narratives do not determine our lives in unilateral fashion, and that ethical responsibility resides in the choices we make over and above social and cultural influences:

> People who believe that they are strong-willed and the masters of their destiny can only continue to believe this by becoming specialists in self-deception. Their decisions are not really decisions at all—a real decision makes one humble, one knows that it is at the mercy of more things than can be named—but elaborate systems of evasion, of illusion, designed to make themselves and the world appear to be what they and the world are not. This is certainly what my decision, made so long ago in Joey's bed, came to.
>
> (Baldwin 2000: 20)

That illusion of "mastery," achieved by "not looking at the universe, by not looking at myself" (Baldwin 2000: 20), depends on David's aggressive and chosen erection of barriers that allow for no disruption of self-hood or possibility of epistemological challenge. Security of a sort is found within a stony, barricaded self.

About his decision finally to move to Paris, David tells us,

> Perhaps, as we say in America, I wanted to find myself. [...] I think now that if I had had any intimation that the self I was going to find would turn out to be only the same self from which I had spent so much time in flight, I would have stayed at home.
>
> (Baldwin 2000: 21)

Of course, David takes his stony self-hating self with him in his travels, as he fearfully allows no avenues for epistemological challenge or any possibility for a macro-perspective on that self. Mae Henderson has rightly termed this a chosen "exile not only from America, but also from self-knowledge" (2005: 304). Thus, even as David discovers a thriving homosexual subculture in Paris, he attempts to remain touristically distant from it, loudly proclaiming his heterosexuality even as he mingles with the exotic "others" whom he alternately exploits and verbally abuses. He accepts money and drinks from anyone who offers but is also quick to ridicule those who fail to meet his conception of normal masculinity. He even allows some of them to give him blow jobs while thinking of "something else" and pretending "that nothing was happening down there in the dark between [his] legs" (Baldwin 2000: 56). For a while, this fiction of emotional self-sufficiency and sham performance of sexual self-mastery persists.

Of course, the point of the novel, written coincidentally at the same time as sections of *Truth and Method,* is much more Gadamerian than David's lingering in such dishonest self-isolation would alone reveal. Allowing himself to follow desire rather than convention, David drifts into an affair with the Italian bartender Giovanni and has then the potentially life-altering opportunity to "find himself," or at least learn something about himself, through interrelationship. That potential for making an active and courageous decision to open up to another is sharpened through ample conversational input. "Love him," his acquaintance Jacques says to David concerning Giovanni: "love him and let him love you. [...] You can give each other something which will make both of you better— forever—if you will *not* be ashamed, if you will only *not* play it safe. [...] You play it safe long enough, [...] and you'll end up trapped in your own dirty body, forever and forever and forever—like me" (Baldwin 2000: 57). Like Gadamer reflecting on failed conversational encounters, the novel thus equates safety with an isolation that is static and even tragic. Responsibility always lies with the individual who can decide to alter his approach to an encounter: "if you think of [your time together] as dirty, then they *will* be dirty; because you will be giving nothing. [...] But you can make your time together anything but dirty" (Baldwin 2000: 57). David's response to Jacques' conversational attempt to shed new light on his "self" is, predictably, silence: "I said nothing" (Baldwin 2000: 57).

Granted, it would be grossly oversimplifying to ascribe to David the possibility of full instrumental agency over his own internalized homophobia. He remains petrified by others' words for what he and the world think of as the "dirty" situation he finds himself in with Giovanni, and responds mechanically and self-protectively: "Inside me something locked. 'I—I cannot have a life with you.' [...] 'What kind of life can two men have together, anyway? All this love you talk about. [...] I'm a man [...] a man. What do you think can *happen* between us?" (Baldwin 2000: 141–2). But even as he asks those pointed questions, to which Giovanni carefully responds, David has made a damning mistake for which the novel does hold him accountable: He has already decided to ignore his interlocutor's perspective. He asks questions rhetorically that are not rhetorical questions. Rather than engage in dialogue, he only declaims monologically. While the novel never denies that David is enveloped in the discourse of American butch masculinity, it reiterates that responsibility lies with an individual who chooses to flee difficult choices, chooses a particular set of relationships and a stance toward those whom he encounters, and chooses to repudiate the perspectives that others shed on the limitations of his own self-conception and self-knowledge.

After all, David makes many active choices; he is no hermit spurning all interactions and relationships, but he seeks through them only to use others for his own narrow and dishonest purposes. He says of his sham heterosexual relationship with Hella,

> I wanted to be inside again, with the light and safety, with my manhood unquestioned, watching my woman put my children to bed. I wanted the same bed at night and the same arms and I wanted to rise in the morning, knowing where I was. I wanted a woman to be for me a steady ground, like the earth itself, where I could always be renewed.
>
> (Baldwin 2000: 104)

That metaphor—of a steady "grounding," of a fixity of gender and sexual definition through an unthinking adherence to tradition—reappears throughout the novel in various permutations. He says he asks Hella to marry him, "to give myself something to be moored to" (Baldwin 2000: 5). She agrees to the marriage because she too wants to be defined narrowly through such a relationship, "I've got you to take care of and feed and torment and trick and love—I've got you to put up with. From now on, I can have a wonderful time complaining about being a woman. But I won't be terrified that I'm *not* one" (Baldwin 2000: 126). Later she wonders, "if women are supposed to be led by men and there aren't any men to lead them, what happens then? What happens then?" (Baldwin 2000: 165). Of course, she does not want an answer to that question, for what would happen "then" is a much more fluid and unpredictable situation involving active decisions over roles and responsibilities. What they imagine achieving through their relationship is a static, nondialogic form of subjectivity, one that stands in stark contrast to the mutuality, mutual challenging, and shared growth that Gadamer implies is the most productive dynamic for interpersonal exchange. This is about as far from the mystical and transcendent as one can imagine.

As I suggested in the preceding chapter, Thomas Alexander finds in Gadamerian theory the possibility for a form of finite transcendence through "loving" relationship with the other. Giovanni is the main spokesperson in the novel for the possibilities of such a transformative experience, one in which erotic partners acquire agency even over the power of cultures to determine unilaterally the meaning of their desire for each other: "If dirty words frighten you, [...] I really don't know how you have managed to live so long. People are full of dirty words. [...] If your countrymen think that privacy is a crime, so much the worse for your country" (Baldwin 2000: 81). "Dirty words" are always subject to tradition-abrading rejoinder in Giovanni's opinion. Yet David will not embrace such loving possibilities and their attendant responsibilities. His response to Giovanni's plea: "I had lost control of the conversation somewhere along the line and I simply wanted it to end" (Baldwin 2000: 82). While even Gadamer never imagines that ideal conversational exchanges are "uncontrolled," David does not allow himself to be challenged and is unwilling to embrace the horizon-shifting dynamism of interlocution. Just as with his sexuality to date, which has centered largely on impassively received oral sex from a man kneeling before him, David remains conversationally impervious and trapped in his own dirty body.

Giovanni's final attempt to break through the barricade is revealing: "You do not [...] love anyone! [...] You love your purity, you love your mirror. [...] You want to be *clean*" (Baldwin 2000: 141). That purity is the false purity of barricaded self-sufficiency, and in ways that hark back to an earlier strand of discussion here, Giovanni ties David's attitude to a particularly impervious form of tourism. Remembering the village in Italy where he was born, Giovanni says:

> I can see you, many years from now, coming through our village in the ugly, fat, American motor car you will surely have by then and looking at me and looking at all of us and tasting our wine and shitting on us with those empty smiles Americans wear everywhere and which you wear all the time and driving off with a great roar of motors and a great sound of tires and telling all the other Americans you meet that they must come and see our village because it is so picturesque. And you will have no idea of the life there, dripping and bursting and beautiful and terrible, as you have no idea of my life now.
>
> (Baldwin 2000: 138–9)

Giovanni challenges an entire mindset of unilateral judgment of and condescension toward the other. As he has throughout the novel, David simply walks out of their last conversation rather than learn anything from it, just as he and the other Americans in the novel are shown to be wholly unwilling to interact with any of their European interlocutors beyond an exploitive and touristic usage of them. Such an unwillingness to listen, learn, and change leads inevitably to tragedy.

David finally destroys Giovanni's life (who is driven to economic desperation and finally murder), he participates in destroying the life of his fiancée who must confront the truth of their sham engagement when she discovers David with a sailor, and he destroys his own seemingly best chance at happiness and growth. Giovanni dies, Hella leaves David, and he is left alone at the novel's end. In its closing paragraphs, he stares at himself in a mirror, thinking "I do not know what moves in this body, what this body is searching. It is trapped in my mirror. [...] I long to crack that mirror and be free" (Baldwin 2000: 168). In Henderson's word, "David, like Narcissus, is trapped in his own self-image, the specular logic of the same" (2005: 315). Of course, the point of the novel and of Gadamer's philosophy too is that the self cannot free the self by itself, and that the only transcendence of self possible is through encounters with other human beings, not through wrangling with an image in a mirror. Baldwin urges us to allow the other to challenge our selfhood, to allow the other to disrupt our self-assurance and our self-esteem, to embrace through the other, the potential for otherness within our selves.

Melting the stone

Feinberg traces a different trajectory, one of mutuality and therefore mutability. I often teach *Giovanni's Room* and *Stone Butch Blues* in dialogue with each other because Jess and David make for a revealing set of contrasts. Jess is far more egregiously abused than David ever was; she is raped, beaten, and subject to a constant barrage of verbal assault for transgressing the same gender norms of 1950s America that David clings to so anxiously. Even so, "Butch" David—however assertive and controlling he may be—is the far more timid character; Jess is both more resilient and more vulnerable, in the sense of allowing others to challenge and change her, even when she is at her most self-enclosed and defensive. While both inhabit a "stoniness" that their novels equate with unhealthy emotional barricades and debilitating fear, she is much more self-aware in that state of defensiveness. David stares in a mirror at the end of his novel, not knowing how to break free from it, while Jess, even as a child, stares in a mirror

> trying to see far in the future. [...] There were no women on tele-vision like the small woman reflected in this mirror, none on the streets. [...] For a moment in that mirror I saw the woman I was growing up to be staring back at me. She looked scared and sad. I wondered if I was brave enough to grow up and be her.
>
> (Feinberg 2003: 20–1)

Brave she proves to be, as she commits to the process that is personal growth through dialogic interaction and epistemological, as well as physical, dislocation. Though hardly living a high-culture suffused, Gadamerian dialogic intellectualism, Jess nevertheless allows for the morphic possibilities of selfhood and belief that Gadamer calls for, as she lives changeability through relationship.

Jess's exteriority to herself, the ability she demonstrates above to reflect upon her selfhood (even if unable to instrumentally alter that selfhood), has ties also to a denaturalization of rigid cultural norms that she experiences in childhood. In her early years, she gravitates toward and is heavily influenced by the culture and beliefs of the Native American women who are her neighbors: "I grew in two worlds, immersed in the music of two languages. One world was Wheaties and Milton Berle. The other was fry bread and sage. One was cold, but it was mine; the other was warm, but it wasn't" (Feinberg 2003: 14). That inbetweenness allows her to hone an ability to place herself imaginatively in the roles and positions occupied by others, evidenced also in her ability even in childhood to sympathize with participants in the early 1960s Civil Rights Movement. Not happy with the self she sees in the mirror, she begins to try on the narratives that others express and live.

Such sympathetic openness, in the service of expanding possible narratives for her own selfhood, is most memorably captured in Jess's self-conscious scripting in dialogue with butches and femmes in the Buffalo queer bar scene. While David is paralyzed by other's words for his situation, Jess is able to work within a supportive micro-community to mold discourse to her and others' purposes. David rejects the creativity, support, and self-altering possibilities of his micro-community in Paris; Jess, just a few years later, eagerly seeks out the same dynamics within Buffalo bar culture, repeatedly and explicitly asking others for instruction: "This was to be our butch 'father to son' talk. Al talked. I listened" (Feinberg 2003: 30). In one of her first sexual encounters, her partner Angie says, "'I'll show you how.' Those were the most comforting words I ever heard," thinks Jess (Feinberg 2003: 71). That Gadamerian foundation of assuming that you have something to learn from the other is the basis of Jess's developing sexual self-awareness and her series of variously successful loving relationships.

Even as *Stone Butch Blues* explores a state of "stony" defensiveness, it is also about a great yearning for connection. Feinberg contextualizes Jess's barricades and reactions in such a way that we always understand their etiology and the potential for connection hiding just beneath the surface of the stony exterior. As Angie says to her during the lovemaking session mentioned above, "Don't be ashamed of being stone with a pro, honey. We're in a stone profession. It's just that you don't have to be stuck in being stone, either. It's OK if you find a femme you can trust in bed" (Feinberg 2003: 73). "You don't have to be stuck" is advice that David rejects but Jess accepts, and what follows is a reciprocation in which Jess "writhed under her touch" (Feinberg 2003: 73), a far different outcome than that portrayed in scenes recounted earlier where Giovanni attempts to challenge David's shame. The stone can melt when openness and trust develops between two partners, and that depends on the decisions made by each.

The novel demonstrates this most memorably in Jess's relationship with Theresa. We might say that Theresa is to Jess what Giovanni could have been to David: the partner best able to melt the stone. Jess writes to her, "You treated my stone self as a wound that needed loving healing. Thank you" (Feinberg 2003: 9). In relationship with Theresa, Jess develops through dialogue and reciprocation: "I grew in leaps and bounds. [...] Most importantly, I learned to say I'm sorry" (Feinberg 2003: 123). Interestingly, Jess learns these lessons so well that she becomes even better than Theresa at embracing ambiguity and rejecting social norms, much as we saw Giovanni advocating. When she decides to transgress the gender binary in a particularly decisive way by having her breasts removed, taking hormones, and attempting to pass as a man, it is Theresa who shuts down: "'Honey, we've got to talk about it,' I said. She sat in silence with me for a long time. Then she got up without a word and went to bed. For weeks we didn't talk about it" (Feinberg 2003: 146–7). That retreat into silence, precipitated this time by Theresa, leads also to a recalcification of Jess: "I turned into one big emotional rock" (Feinberg 2003: 147). When they do eventually talk again, earnestly and openly, it is to end their relationship. Theresa wants Jess to remain visibly on the female side of the binary man/woman because she is afraid of what others will think. Jess feels a core need to attempt life as a man whatever Theresa thinks. This impasse reminds us that dialogue as I have explored it here does not lead necessarily or regularly to consensus, nor should it. Dialogue is simply key to enhanced understanding. Theresa and Jess part forever, each understanding the basis of the other's needs and beliefs, even if unable to bridge their divides. That is not failure in Gadamerian terms; it is the hard dissensual work that is the basis for all responsible and responsive living.

"I'm listening. I'll think about it" (Feinberg 2003: 139) are words Jess expresses in various ways many times in the novel, and they are key to understanding her divergence from David's more static emotional and intellectual state. "When I sat alone and asked what it was I really wanted, the answer was *change*," Jess says (Feinberg 2003: 224). Other individuals are agents helping drive that change process, and she is able to learn from their successes and failures. David may ignore Jacques' warning about his future, but Jess remarks, "When I was a kid I looked at Al and I saw my future in her. I looked at her today and thought maybe that's my future, too. [...] I was thinking about Edwin's suicide, too. [...] Maybe I was afraid her suicide was my future" (Feinberg 2003: 290). That ability to wrestle with possible futurities, bound up with critical reflection on others' narratives, differentiates her story dramatically from that of David. "What kind of life can we have in this room?—this filthy little room. What kind of life can two men have together anyway?" (Baldwin 2000: 142), David asks in his typically closed-ended rhetorical fashion. Jess is much better able to test possible futures—some desirable and some fearful—through dialogic exchange and then thank her interlocutors for their assistance in helping her sort out the different possibilities, saying finally to her mentor Al, "I loved you then and I love you now. [...] I love you" (Feinberg 2003: 289). These are words that never come out of David's mouth to Giovanni or Jacques. David shuts down by saying, in effect, "no future." Jess wants a future over which she exercises whatever agency she can discover.

And this same projective dialogic openness is fundamental as well to Jess's political growth and especially her interactions with the union activist Duffy, who says to her "I really do believe we can change the world. [...] I'm not saying we'll live to see some sort of paradise. Take a chance, Jess. You're already wondering if the world could change. Try imagining a world worth living in, and then ask yourself if that isn't worth fighting for." "I got to think about all of this" is her characteristically open response (Feinberg 2003: 299). Duffy's call for a provisional utopianism of the sort I discussed in Chapter 2 is given particular prominence because it is repeated at the novel's end, just before the penultimate words "I closed my eyes and allowed my hopes to soar" (Feinberg 2003: 301). *Giovanni's Room* ends with David's ripped-up missive from Jacques concerning Giovanni blowing back into his face at a moment of a daybreak that "weighs" on his shoulders; *Stone Butch Blues* ends with newly released birds soaring, like dreams, into the dawn. One is centrifugal, the other centripetal.

David remains characteristically silent as Giovanni is put to death. Jess's narrative culminates in her finding a public voice for herself at a political rally in New York: "This is what courage is. It's not just living through a nightmare, it's doing something with it afterward. It's being brave enough to talk about it to other people" (Feinberg 2003: 296). And talk Jess does, publicly embracing the gender transgressive category of "a butch, a he-she" (Feinberg 2003: 296), no doubt a "dirty word" in David's lexicon. Her articulations touch others in the crowd even as they also expose her to the possibility of ridicule and retaliation. Yet she lives thereby the Gadamerian injunction: to be brave enough to commit to the dialogue that will expose your self, that will change your self, and that may change the selves of others as a consequence of dialogue. Unlike David in his dead-ended trip to Paris, Jess' life- and consciousness-altering journeys—to Buffalo and its bar culture and then to New York City and a loving relationship with her transgendered neighbor Ruth—allow for movement through an expanded number of conversational encounters and other forms of self-disruption. She welcomes those challenges, and, through them, she is finally able to embrace the future.

That is the great opportunity offered by all forms of travel and encounters with difference, and not simply ones that lead to erotic relationship. As I will explore in my next chapter, such opportunities may be diminishing as consumerism and Anglo-American discourses of gender, sexuality, and consumption-based identity circulate across the globe. Of course, to the extent that there is an ongoing process of epistemological and cultural homogenization, it is one that travelers themselves participate in and is something that I am hardly innocent of (working with Peace Corps, showing videos of American news broadcasts to my students and using textbooks whose references included American pop culture and history). Yet there are always ethical choices, even as there are no pure motives and no level playing fields for global, or even more local, encounters. The ethical choice is certainly not isolationism and sterile interiority. The ethical choice, following Gadamer and Feinberg and Baldwin, is recognizing that perhaps the other is right, to allow the other to change one's self.

Leaving and learning

And that returns me to my initial "maybe, sort of" answer to whether travel is a mystical and transcendental experience. It is not supernatural because it is thoroughly rooted in the human and, ideally, the humane. Yet transcendental ... sort of. It is impure and compromised but it is potentially, finitely transcendental in its disruption of our self-satisfaction and epistemological security. Certainly, I have been changed by travel and more permanent forms of dislocation—irrevocably and in ways I never could have predicted. That two-year teaching visit to Rwanda was preceded by an even more fundamentally life-altering decision three years earlier to leave Alabama behind forever. The chance discovery of *The Happy Hooker* that I discussed in Chapter 1 did not lead immediately to my packing my bags, running away, and seeking adventure; I was far too timid to think of becoming a runaway after having seen innumerable television movies and series episodes detailing the horrors of life on the street for homeless adolescents (*Dawn: Portrait of a Teenage Runaway* and its sequel *Alexander: The Other Side of Dawn* probably scared into temporary conformity a whole generation of 1970s youth).

But I did leave eventually. Capitulating to my parents' demand that I stay relatively close to home when I went to college, I raced through a University of Alabama BA program and then packed my bags and moved to join a female friend who had taken a cheap apartment in New York City a year earlier. Nineteen-eighties New York grittiness and sexual openness (traced so accurately and lovingly by Samuel Delany in *Times Square Red, Times Square Blue* and destroyed so violently and stupidly by Rudy Giuliani's Disneyfication of the city by the century's end) changed and expanded my horizons in innumerable ways. While I'll write about more recent Los Angeles-based sex club culture in Chapter 5, New York's sex venues (as timidly as I approached and participated in them in 1981 and 1982) were places of conversation, camaraderie, and narrative generation. Everyone had a story to tell—just as they did in the bars that I also frequented—everyone (almost) was from somewhere else and loved to tell the tale of escape from Nebraska, Louisiana, Utah, and Alabama. Where we were from and where we wanted to go were the subjects of intense conversations in bars, lounge areas, and locker rooms. In those years before MySpace, YouTube, and web chat rooms we found each other and we expanded each other's horizons because we had decided to leave behind the known and embrace the strangeness and diversity of New York. Like Jess, we desperately wanted to learn as much as possible about and from others; our narratives intersected, as we complicated and altered each other's futures. Of course those venues were danger-filled also, in ways we did not know then, because of the imminent HIV crisis (and I'll have more to say on that later), but what matters most here is that we were willing to risk our sense of who we were and who we had been to date by seeking out others from whom to ask and learn about different possible sexual selfhoods. Every time I reread *Stone Butch Blues* it reinforces my experience that if we make the fundamental choice to listen carefully as well as speak openly (to the extent that we can—and certainly that extent can be highly compromised by material deprivation, trauma, and other factors), we are also empowered to make innumerable subsequent choices as we sort through the proffered lessons and possibilities.

Even in small-town West Virginia, a life-altering, life-enhancing conversation continues for me in face-to-face and mediated encounters, as I will continue to affirm. The Gadamerian meeting and fusion of horizons is always possible, even when we cannot or do not choose to move physically across regional, national, and cultural borders. When we can and choose to do so, the possibilities multiply exponentially. Our own class and gender positions and certainly American economic, media-cultural, and military power make these dynamics far from balanced and fair, but that inequality points to an even greater need for the sensitivity, openness, and self-destabilization that Gadamer calls for. Like David, too many of us in the Western world have been looking in the mirror for too long, defensive about and protective of our supposed "purity."

This is true as well for the field of "queer theory," theory that can be pure in its too-frequent inapplicability to daily life, pure in its sometimes tediously self-referential nature, and too often thoroughly closed to the otherness around and potentially within us. In interjecting philosophical hermeneutics into the current discussion in sexuality studies, what I am calling for is an opening up of the corpus of theoretical work that we reference and for us to allow difference to disrupt the sanctity of our worldviews. This demands a conscious choice on the part of those participating in the field to move outside a zone of self-assurance and comfort, to allow epistemological and phenomenological challenges to occur, and to return to the self with a usefully complicated and altered understanding of the self and its place in a world of selves. As a group of intellectuals and activists, we need to be less like David and more like Jess. Certainly when I re-read *Giovanni's Room*, I do so with the desire to test myself against it, to make sure that David's stone butch blues do not provide the soundtrack to my life.

Openness, then, means loving difference more than sameness, loving heterogeneity more than homogeneity. In the wicked sense I mentioned previously, it means embracing the hetero and repudiating the homo. My hermeneutics of travel, my queer philosophical hermeneutics, is exuberantly "hetero" theory; what we should love about traveling through this queer world—temporally and geographically—is the hetero-ness of it. As Baldwin and Feinberg urge, we need to love and listen to the hetero around us if we are going to allow it to transform the homo within all of us.

4 Global conversations

In an essay that addresses many of the factors that mitigate against productive conversation among American academics, Jane Tompkins and Gerald Graff ask "Can We Talk?" as a titular question and then speak about their fears and hopes in a series of written exchanges. Jane is skeptical from the outset:

> No, not very well. Too many things get in the way.
> Pride [...] and envy, for example. Academic people are afraid they might make a mistake, or not have all of the evidence they need, or not look smart or have all of the good arguments on their side; so they keep quiet. They're afraid to risk what they really think for fear they'll get shot down.
>
> (Tompkins and Graff 2001: 21)

Jerry doesn't disagree with her assessment of the severity of the problem but traces the root cause to a different culprit:

> I gather that you see the lack of good discussion as a feature of our professional culture, whereas I see it as a local condition of campus life. [...] What curtails and blocks discussion, it seems to me, is a local institutional structure that keeps people isolated and contains few arenas in which discussion can take place—or rather contains that discussion within the cozy confines of in-groups that endlessly reinforce our pet prejudices while protecting ourselves from the criticism of outsiders.
>
> (Tompkins and Graff 2001: 22)

The various difficulties that they isolate (which they finally acknowledge as overdetermining conversational impasses in the academy) increase exponentially when one moves beyond the relative homogeneity of the

American college campus and out into the world of dramatic and some-times overwhelming global differences: linguistic, religious, economic, racial, and sexual. Our fears of "not looking smart" and the comfort we derive from cozy in-group structures often render our attempts at widely cast, cross-cultural dialogue stilted, halfhearted, or even wholly paralyzed by anxiety. Our pet prejudices concerning different cultures and sexual epistemologies are, indeed, endlessly reinforced.

Yet the question asked by Tompkins and Graff—can we talk?—takes on a heightened, even life-and-death, urgency when posed internationally, though given the skepticism and hostile retrenchment that often attends such a request, perhaps the more important questions are "can we listen?" and "can we learn from what we hear?" The image of David from *Giovanni's Room* as he stares silently at his own reflection in a mirror should haunt us all with its implication of a cultural narcissism that is at once static and destructive. I will argue in the coming pages that an unsettling challenge or discomforting query is not something we should avoid or fear; rather, it is that which we should invite and eagerly await. Only the other can free the self from the trap of interiority and profound mistake. And in turn, it is that self's responsibility to reciprocate with care and sensitivity.

Silence

In July of 2006 I traveled to a major international humanities conference in Tunisia that offered a venue where cross-cultural and cross-disciplinary conversations could be initiated in an environment of respect and common quest for understanding. I successfully proposed to the organizing committee a ninety-minute session entitled "A Conversation and Workshop on Queer Studies in a Global Context," which appeared in the program with the descriptor "Following a brief theoretical introduction, this workshop will offer participants the opportunity to engage in conversations about the future directions of queer sexuality studies in a diverse global context." For the workshop, I planned to deliver a short overview of Gadamerian theory and the utility of utopian thinking, and then prepared for distribution a one-page handout and discussion starter that included various headings and prompts, querying participants on their thoughts regarding globalization and traditional sexual identities, transgender identities and human rights, and religion and sexuality, among other topics.

I hoped for a lively exchange that would lead to increased understanding and mutual respect across cultures on sexual diversity issues.

No one showed up. Or rather a few people did—all of whom were almost exactly like me. We were five people, all from the USA, Canada, or Australia, and all of us waiting expectantly for someone "different" to walk into the room and challenge our worldviews or preconceptions. No one ever did. We certainly had a pleasant conversation about our home institutions and hopes for the future, but we were such a homogenous group that we might as well have been sitting at a disciplinary conference in Chicago or Toronto, surrounded by fast-food chains and sports bars, instead of a suburb of Tunis surrounded by mosques and date palms. As a cross-cultural encounter and conversation, it seemed an abysmal failure.

I was very naive. The several hundred conference participants included well over 100 academics and activists from North and sub-Saharan Africa, the Middle East, East and Southeast Asia, and South America, but I had failed to ask myself why anyone who wasn't already comfortable with the discourse and base-level assumptions common to "queer studies" as it is defined largely by the American academy would want to show up to reveal and discuss their disagreements. I wasn't wrong in attempting to create a venue for conversation, but certainly my discourse of "queerness" was discordant and exclusionary, and my expectations were wildly inflated. Almost twenty-five years after my Peace Corps experience I still had a lot of the same "middle-class American white guy" assumptions that once again needed to be exposed as such. Some lessons need to be relearned regularly.

Moreover, some preliminary questions need to be asked more explicitly. How can we begin to talk productively and sensitively about sexuality in a global context when sex tourism still thrives and when Americans and Europeans are all too regularly caught traveling to Southeast Asia to exploit Cambodian and Laotian children? How can we talk about queer sexuality without rancor when those horrific images from Abu Ghraib showing American men and women sexually humiliating and torturing Iraqis linger like the stench of death over any attempt at cross-cultural dialogue? How can we converse on sexual freedom of expression "in the digital age" when over one half of the world lives, or attempts to live, on less than two dollars per day? When world communities still disagree bitterly on allowable roles for men and women, how can we even begin to speak about the rights of the transgendered? How can we talk about desire across differences, when those differences have fed desires for geographic conquest, economic exploitation, and enslavement? Does Gadamer help at all when we are dealing with traditions of horrific abuse and continuing hatred and distrust?

I think he does, and I also believe that we can commit ourselves to the daunting process of initiating and attempting to sustain cross-cultural dialogue even knowing that we will make mistakes, look foolish, and suffer setbacks. Frankly, to do otherwise is to value our self-image and pride more than our quest for understanding and perhaps our collective survival.

Complicating Gadamer for global dialogue

This is not to claim a universal applicability for Gadamer or any other theorist. If we demand an easy and uniformly applicable formula for global dialogue, then we will inevitably be disappointed or forced into error. Gadamer allows us only one possible starting point, not an end point or perfect mechanism, for conversation. His is a voice in a conversation on difference and mutuality that demands careful attention but also consideration as always imperfect and historically/culturally situated. Even so, in times of vicious conflict and political recalcitrance, Gadamer reminds us to involve ourselves enthusiastically in a process over which we have no determining power. As importantly, he reminds us that our views and values will be, must be, as thoroughly interrogated as those views and values which we wish to challenge and potentially change. It is for this reason that Mae Henderson finds Gadamer's emphasis on reciprocity and respect for difference "useful and productive" for discussing black women's struggles, because Gadamer validates "tradition in the subdominant order" as it "constitutes an operative challenge to the dominant order" (Henderson 1992: 147). Veronica Vasterling, writing also on the applicability of Gadamer to power-laden relationships and disputes, notes that one can find in Gadamer a useful recognition of the "alienness, strangeness, [and] difference of cultures and worldviews" (2003: 164); philosophical hermeneutics tempers our hope for an eventual fusion of all global horizons because of the "incommensurable evaluative standards" (2003: 167) that would render such fusion elusive if not impossible. Vasterling cites the dispute over whether clitoridectomy constitutes "mutilation of the body" or "cultural identity" (2003: 166) as an instance in which an understanding of the terms of the other's position may be possible, but agreement on a common conclusion impossible to achieve. Yet what she holds out as commendable, even in such a state of impasse, is this: "only open dialogue can actually help us to recognize [...] the real, irreducible plurality of evaluative standards and, hence, the disturbing otherness of the other who challenges my worldview and my conception of the good life" (Vasterling 2003: 167). This is an instance of dissensus in action, as I discussed it earlier. However deeply felt Vasterling's point of view is as a feminist working out of a Western notion of identity politics, she argues that the other's point of view, even on an issue such as clitoridectomy, must be heard and treated with respect. Greater understanding in a dis-sensual global conversation is often the best we can hope for, and such understanding is something that silence or antagonistic engagement—dialogue's likely alternatives—would never foster.

For queer and other radical activists, one can immediately imagine the limit cases where our patience and ability to respect the other's dif-fering "evaluative standards" are sorely tried. Fred Phelp's "Army of God" protesters screaming for the obliteration of homosexuals and homosexuality, judges meting out Shariah-law based death penalties for same-sex lovers in Iran and Nigeria, and bat or tire-iron wielding bash-ers attacking gender and sexual nonconformists in Estonia, St. Maarten, and New York City, hardly embody a worldview or form of cultural expression that one would find worthy of respectful disagreement. However, without the impulse to understand the other's worldview, even in cases as horrific as those, we are left only with anger and vio-lence as a redress. The Gadamerian injunction remains: to let the other's point of view, even when radically different from our own—especially when radically different from our own—spur us onward in our quest for greater understanding. The other's refusal of or indifference to an offer of conversational engagement never lessens our own responsibility for continued, attempted understanding. Hurt, anger, or outrage, even when warranted by the horrific nature of the other's action, is monologic and must, over time, give way to a more nuanced and dialogic stance or it is embittering, static, and self-destructive.

Gadamerian theory would urge us then to articulate a utopia of earn-est and productive global interaction, one of respect for difference among and within nations and cultures, and for a fusion of horizons that encompasses all human diversity within the horizon of valued human life. But as motivational as that ideal may be—and as necessary as it is for many of us working in queer academics/activism—we have to think of it as provisional only because it is a projection out of our own standpoint epistemologies and situated understandings. Fusion is by definition not supplantation. If we do not welcome change in our selves through the process of dialogic interaction with the other, then that process is actually one of attempted imposition of our worldviews on the other. That is not Gadamerian dialogics or fusion; that is colonization. I remember an instance from the same Tunisian conference that I mention above in which an American academic haughtily dismissed the claims of a Tunisian professor teaching in Saudi Arabia who said she found wearing an *abaya* and veil "liberating because of the anonymity that it provides." For the American academic, her Muslim interlocutor was simply stupid and wrong in her perspective whatever her experiences and sense of selfhood were. Needless to say, the conversation ended abruptly and uncomfortably with that summary reading of the other's life.

Cross-cultural engagement on questions of identity politics cannot have as its practical goal conversion. Sexual radicals have been the object of conversion demands for centuries, so we should be the most skeptical about any process of forcing another into a change of underlying belief or perspective. As difficult as it will be for us to stomach or accept, we have to be willing to talk with all others, even those who think we are evil, inhuman, criminal, or mentally ill. While obviously we must self-protect, we must also remember that any revulsion we may feel in interacting with people whose perspectives appall us is no doubt matched by the level of physical and psychological discomfort felt by those interlocutors. The Gadamerian process always demands of us that we recognize and appreciate the power of the traditions that have formed others, and in doing so, gain some critical awareness of our own perspectives. We may find the other's traditions to be riddled with prejudices of the most appalling sort, but in understanding those traditions and their origins, we are better able to communicate effectively with those who cling tenaciously to them. The practical and mundane goal of our conversations must be enhanced understanding, even if our long-term provisional utopia is much more ambitiously transformative of both self and other.

Even such a modest goal as "enhanced understanding" still presents enormous challenges, of course. Effective conversation depends on a certain translatability of beliefs and perspectives, so that no matter how divergent two horizons might be, they can at least meet and metamorphose through linguistic contact. This is especially difficult when the language backgrounds of the interlocutors are dissimilar. Not only is the translatability of concepts problematic when moving among Russian, Arabic, English, Korean, and Kiswahili, but we also encounter the problem that Tompkins mentions above of "fear" that we will look foolish in even attempting to speak across language divides, especially if our skills in a particular foreign language are modest (I am always horribly self-conscious when speaking French or German because I think I sound stupid). However, we have to value the process over our own sense of pride and love the adventure of the attempt, even with the many imperfections and embarrassments that we will encounter. There is no linguistic safe zone unless we remain firmly barricaded within the silos that Graff alludes to above (and, really, not even there). Attempting to speak across cultural boundaries can be enormously challenging, but our commitment to activist engagement must override our academic self-consciousness or desire for perfect expression. These are challenges that we can continue to confront and imperfectly negotiate over and through as we attempt to translate our thoughts and words into another language, have them translated for us, or negotiate to find a third language—not ours, not the interlocutor's—that allows an imperfect medium for conversational exchange. I speak no Spanish or Italian, so when traveling to Spain or Italy, I resort to my "stupid" French to make myself understood, often a second (or third or fourth) language of my interlocutor. Conversation is not impossible given global linguistic diversity, only— occasionally—excruciating.

A second challenge is, of course, the one I encountered in Tunis: What happens if we attempt to initiate a conversation but find no interlocutor immediately interested in responding? Gadamer's life provides an example that is helpful here. In 1981, the Goethe Institute in Paris orchestrated an "encounter" between Gadamer and Jacques Derrida that was supposed to be a cross-cultural exchange on contrasts between French and German philosophy as represented by the two invited speakers. As is documented superbly in Michelfelder and Palmer's *Dialogue and Deconstruction* (1989), Gadamer acquainted himself thoroughly with Derridean theory and delivered a long and thoughtful address that revealed his perspectives on the divergences and convergences of their two philosophical stances. Derrida, on the other hand, ignored Gadamer, ignored the request for "exchange," and simply delivered a brief lecture on Nietzsche and Heidegger that signaled no interest in a conversation with his would-be interlocutor. The "encounter" seemed like an abysmal failure.

However, it was not, and neither was my Tunisian experience, when one expands the notion of conversation longitudinally. Attendees of the Gadamer/Derrida (non)event spoke endlessly about the experience. It has resulted in Michelfelder and Palmer's collection of compelling essays and in cogent analysis in many subsequent works examining the two writers' careers. I am writing about it here, of course. Their (non)conversation has been thus the subject of continuing subsequent conversations. Similarly, the (non)event of my Tunisian workshop became the springboard for many discussions over lunches, dinners, and coffee hours at the conference, with many interlocutors of various nationalities and perspectives (all of whom offered useful readings of what didn't happen: too many parallel panels, shyness at the prospect of talking about sexuality, concerns that the theory base would be overly specialized, and simple lack of interest in the topic). I have spoken with a variety of people about the (non)event since the conference and am writing about it here. Even silence is a form of dialogic intervention, one that can become a springboard for the next attempt at interlocution. If dialogue is the phenomenological basis of life itself, as I am suggesting throughout this book, then the page before you is an instance of a dialogue that includes what happened or didn't happen in Tunisia. My (non)event was simply a little stumbling point in what is a rich, ever-expanding conversation.

Reading queer globalization theory for dialogic possibilities

Queer scholars have begun adding their voices to that exchange on global sexual differences and from a variety of perspectives. Essay collections, journal issues, and conference panels on the topic abound now, and some of them invite conversational rejoinders here as they speak to the parameters and consequences of cross-cultural dialogue. Clearly they signal that the current breadth of the conversation is considerable, even if that breadth is itself a subject worthy of some debate. For example, in their introductory words to the collection *Queer Globalizations: Citizenship and the Afterlife of Colonialism*, Arnaldo Cruz-Malavé and Martin F. Manalansan IV announce, "Queerness is now global. Whether in advertising, film, performance art, the Internet, or the political discourses of human rights in emerging democracies, images of queer sexualities and cultures now circulate around the globe" (Cruz-Malavé and Manalansan 2002: 1). There is something a bit triumphal in that declaration, and I am far less comfortable than they are with "queerness" assuming global ubiquity. The term, its denotations, and connotations still circulate primarily among members of the privileged classes and those with Western media and internet access. Queerness is not global if we include in the "global" subsistence farmers, the illiterate, most North Koreans and Saudis (who do not have unrestricted access to the web or other media), and innumerable others who do not participate in what the writers above take as another global given: "capitalist market exchange" (Cruz-Malavé and Manalansan 2002: 2) and the purchase of "gay and lesbian lifestyle products" (2002: 1). Yet certainly if we take "global" to indicate rather more loosely a widely circulating concept that crosses many national boundaries, then queerness is arguably global in its grasp, given the colonizing, or at least overwriting, effect that Western, capital-backed, and media-disseminated discourse can have in its interactions with other traditions and classificatory schemas.

Admittedly, my own choice of term is problematic here: "grasp" implies a specific intentionality (and personification) that does not do full justice to the complexity of flows of power, capital, and discourse. Yes, there are grasping and exploitive people who cause harm in their interactions with people from other nations and cultures, but there are countless others (myself included) who unwittingly participate in processes and paradigm shifts that have unintended but no doubt deleterious effects (I do not know where all the money that I have placed in my savings account has been reinvested and to what effect). Ascriptions of intentionality tend to binarize individuals and groups without prompting any understanding of the complexity of the other's standpoint epistemology and perspective. I have certainly been guilty of this at times (and am well aware that I am testy and impatient with works such as *No Future*) and Cruz-Malavé and Manalansan may demonstrate a similarly polarized/polarizing view in a complicated anecdote they relate in the introduction to their essay collection. In a question-and-answer period at the conference from which the collection's papers were drawn, a white (in their words), "well-meaning U.S. queer scholar of note" asked an "earnest" question of a conference panel made of up scholars of color (Cruz-Malavé and Manalansan 2002: 3). He had been approached recently in a public park by a self-identifying "ex-gay" Latino who attempted to give him religious literature. Taken aback by anyone claiming to be cured of homosexuality through religion, he asked the panelists, "How should I have spoken to this Latino man? How could I have made myself understood by him?" (Cruz-Malavé and Manalansan 2002: 3). An uncomfortable silence followed as no one knew how to answer the question. Clearly the scholar was offensive in his expectation that a panel of non-white scholars could speak authoritatively about a difficult and complicated situation involving another non-Caucasian. Yet even with the luxury of time, the editors' response was silence and silencing: "This anthology on queer globalizations is our insistent attempt not to answer the white scholar's query, deflecting thus his colonizing gaze" (Cruz-Malavé and Manalansan 2002: 4). A "well-meaning" question about how to engage in conversation—even a stupid question—is not colonization. In fact, I would argue that we don't need fewer questions—stupid, smart, or somewhere in between—we need more.

In the words of Silviano Santiago, one of their contributors, even insensitive questions are pregnant moments of dialogue, one charged with the opportunity "to raise the inquirer's awareness with respect to his or her utterance—an utterance charged with politically hegemonic values" (Santiago 2002: 13). He notes, "there is a moment of mediation in dialogue, and [...] that moment should be allowed to speak" (2002: 14), because if that moment of always imperfect translatability and heavily weighted participation in interlocution is denied or suppressed, we are locked in opposing camps in which nothing can be learned by anyone present. As I have suggested throughout this book, we all speak out of our own standpoint epistemologies, and only by learning to place our own limitations in conversation with those of others can we gain a measure of leverage over the processes that occur without intent and also potentially without a critical awareness that, if acquired, might lead to a reshaping or revision. Speaking at the other without listening to the other leads only to the distrust that resulted from the Tunisian (non) exchange on wearing the *abaya* and veil. Speaking about an insensitive, questioning scholar or other interlocutor without conversing with him or her, when the opportunity is there and pregnant with possibility, accomplishes little beyond deepened distrust and a heightened fear of looking foolish.

This hardly means that we should fail to recognize and be wary of the potential for the colonizing impact of the perspectives of privileged-class gays and lesbians from the USA and Europe. Roberto Strongman argues that "the exportation of [Western] knowledges on sexual orientation has a universalizing and homogenizing effect that erases culturally distinct and politically enabling gender differences in poorer populations and among communities of color worldwide" (2002: 176). Language and cultural sensitivity are enormously important in participating in cross-cultural dialogue on sexual and gender diversity. "Gay" and "lesbian" simply do not translate seamlessly into the experiences and self-identifications of individuals across the state of West Virginia, much less the globe. No one has been a more widely cited and insistent critic of this dynamic than Dennis Altman, whose book *Global Sex* includes a thoughtful critique of the colonizing force of American queer culture as it interacts with economically disadvantaged groups and non-privileged discourses. In Altman's words, "'Modern' ways of being homosexual threaten not only the custodians of 'traditional' morality, they also threaten the position of 'traditional' forms of homosexuality" (2001: 88). He thus echoes Manalansan, who in an essay predating the collection above observed cogently that the term "gay" itself depends on "a developmental narrative that begins with an unliberated, 'prepolitical' homosexual practice and that culminates in a liberated, 'out,' politicized, 'modern,' 'gay' subjectivity" (Manalansan 1997: 487). Strongman too calls for a renewed commitment to opposing "total domination by the hegemonic master narrative of gay liberation in favor of more culturally pertinent form options" (2002: 189). Yet clearly the answer cannot be hermetically sealing off cultures from all external influences. Not only is that an impossibility, it is also a version of the static self-absorption that doomed David to error and isolation.

Discursive negotiations over competing "narratives"—ones offering differing modes of self-identification and political coalitional possibilities—are themselves a form of dialogue. This is not to deny the heavy and oppressive force of market creation, consumerism, tourism, and economic exploitation that can drive the overlay of Euro-American categories across the globe. Altman is convincing in his indictment of "the dominance of the American imaginary [evidenced] in the proliferation across the world of bars and restaurants and discos with American names. One current gay guide lists the Disco Hollywood on Ghengis Khan Avenue, Ulan Bator" (2001: 29). But other voices in the conversation on globalized sexualities dissent from Altman's model of unilateral imposition. Kenyan writer John Mburu counters that such identity overlays can (and must be encouraged to) coexist with traditional epistemologies:

> By claiming a multifaceted and multilayered identity, as Africans and as gays and lesbians, we hope to confront the formidable challenges before us. The pervasive ideology that still portrays homosexuality as un-African and Western can only be neutralized by an ideal that embraces Africa's various traditions and customs as well as the Western influences that are now an indelible part of Africa's traditions as well.
>
> (Mburu 2000: 189)

Jon Binnie concurs in saying,

> We need to redress the balance in queer commentaries on globalization in focusing on sexual dissidents as active producers and workers, not simply passive consumers as they are commonly represented in political economic accounts of queer consumption. [... We] cannot simply dismiss the desire of many sexual dissidents to embrace a global gay identity as a form of false consciousness.
>
> (Binnie 2004: 60)

To read the other simply as a "dupe" of Anglo-American discourse and media is to deny her or him the ability to make active choices and to speak and act authoritatively out of a standpoint epistemology worthy of inherent respect.

To avoid the neo-colonialism inherent in reading the other as misguided and/or stupid (performing a multiculturalist's version of the above-mentioned summary reading offered by the American academic of veil-wearing Tunisians), a growing body of nuanced work uses as its model a form of dialogism among identity categories and cultures regarding sexual diversity. Peter Drucker asserts:

> It is all too easy to conclude that because people read a European book, watch a US video, or wear the same kind of leather jacket you could see in a Sydney bar, their identities and lives are the same. [...]

Local and global imagery and identities are in constant, sometimes contradictory, sometimes complementary interaction.

(Drucker 2000: 26–7)

In rejecting "the notion that globalization means the homogenization of queer culture" (Binnie 2004: 60), Binnie and Drucker would not deny the fact that the weighty force of Anglo-American-European identity categories and consumption-based notions of lifestyle do alter local and traditional ways of being and knowing. However, they would counter that cultures have always been responsive to external forces. Processes of cultural change are not ones only of loss but also of invention and imaginative rejoinder. Mexican activist Max Mejía captures that interactivity in noting that

Mexicans' perceptions of homosexuality today include noticeable cultural influences from the contemporary globalized world. But they also include noticeable influences from remote culture, inherited from pre-Hispanic times, with their particular understanding of homosexuality, as well as noticeable influences from the Christianity brought by the conquerors, with its vision of "the infamous sin."

(Mejía 2000: 43)

This is not "hybridity" as that term is used at times to indicate a uniformity of produced vision or a single "fused" perspective. It is instead a pastiche and continuing interplay of identity categories, desires, traditions, and prejudices that certainly lead to alterations over time, but never a drab, uniform synthetic product. Cultural and sexual distinctions still abound even in the process of cross-cultural exchange and change. Certainly some voices in a global conversation are louder and more imposing than others. For those speaking from a position of privilege, therefore, the injunction to listen carefully and to remain open to challenge is particularly weighty.

Reading global queer rights and the Yogyakarta Principles

Conversation is never pure or on perfectly equal footing; it will always involve calibrations of perceived hierarchies and filtering processes as we speak and listen from within our own horizons. Our awareness of that complexity should produce neither resignation nor cynicism but instead provide much of the base matter of our conversations about difference and dialogism. It is a conversation that should lead to new forms of understanding. As a case in point, two major international organizations have been pointedly critiqued for their Euro-American centrism in the past. The ILGA (International Lesbian and Gay Association) and the IGLHRC (International Gay and Lesbian Human Rights Commission) are both headquartered in the Northern and Western Hemispheres (ILGA in Brussels and IGLHRC in New York) and clearly (as evidenced in their names) adopt American/European identity categories in their worldviews and as organizing principles. Manalansan has been particularly critical of the elitism of such organizations with their mega-conferences and glitzy events that financially preclude participation by people from the developing world and less privileged class backgrounds (see Manalansan 1997: 486–93). In response, both organizations have made important moves in recent years to diversify their membership base and pay close attention to class and racial diversity issues, though they remain plagued by their impulse to "promote a universal language of identity politics" (Altman 2001: 126). While the promotion of basic human rights in ways that include sexual diversity is laudable, any attendant promotion of a "universal language" carries with it heavy baggage and incites understandable skepticism among those whose languages are degraded or erased by the supposedly "universal." This is not to deny the important work done by either organization (I am a member of both and find especially useful their action alerts on death-penalty cases and imminent repressive moves by governments); however, their "speaking position" is always going to be suspect because of the universalizing impact of their titular identity categories.

Other recent international efforts have had diversity and linguistic suppleness at their core and tread more carefully than ILGA or IGLHRC in the use of language and modes of identification (of self and other). A remarkable case in point are the Yogyakarta Principles, which provide the most persuasive and high-profile international human-rights effort to date in claiming gender diversity and sexual orientational freedom as core principles within international law and shared human experience. Developed at Gadjah Mada University in Yogyakarta, Indonesia at a summit held from November 6–9 2006, the principles were publicly released in March of 2007. The summit was made up of twenty-nine jurists and human-rights specialists representing all parts of the globe. Participants from the USA, Britain, Australia and New Zealand numbered only seven of the twenty-nine, with Europe accounting for another eight (and of those, four were representatives from Poland, Serbia, Bulgaria, and Moldova—not traditional "Western" powers). The remaining fourteen were human-rights commissioners, judges, and attorneys from Argentina, Turkey, Pakistan, India, Botswana, Thailand, Costa Rica, Indonesia, China, Nepal, South Africa, Brazil, and Kenya (which sent two representatives). The gathering was gender and linguistically diverse, though admittedly homogenous in other ways since all participants were members of the legal, civil service, or NGO professions.

In choosing the title "The Yogyakarta Principles," the summit participants, their co-chairs (Sonia Onufer Corrêa of Brazil and Vitit Muntarbhorn of Thailand), and rapporteur (Michael O'Flaherty of Ireland) clearly sought to locate the summit's internal work and international agenda outside of the hegemonic space of the USA or Western Europe. Similarly, the thirty-five-page document explaining the twenty-nine adopted principles, as well as the peripheral materials (such as press releases and "backgrounders"), commonly avoid using terms such as "gay," "lesbian," or "queer" so as to delink the work of the summit from the linguistic/cultural colonization of regional or local sexual identities by Anglo-American categories (the rare exception to that is in the preamble and the infrequent citing of specific examples of discrimination and harassment in which such terms are arguably contextually appropriate). As indicated in the document's subtitle—"Principles on the Application of International Human Rights Law in Relation to Sexual Orientation and Gender Identity"—the summit participants deploy the language of orientation and identity without attempting to name the many specific variants that might be included. Thus, the document avoids the laundry list of LGBTQ that inevitably excludes far more than it can ever embrace. While "orientation" is an admittedly controversial concept, Sara Ahmed has argued convincingly for its broad utility in locating peoples and their desires in time and space (Ahmed 2006: 2–24). For the Yogyakarta summit participants, it represented a pragmatic choice of terminology.

The Principles themselves are full of such pragmatic, though also inevitably problematic, choices. The document's base level definitions of two key terms read as such:

1. Sexual orientation is understood to refer to each person's capacity for profound emotional, affectional and sexual attraction to, and intimate and sexual relations with, individuals of a different gender or the same gender or more than one gender.
2. Gender identity is understood to refer to each person's deeply felt internal and individual experience of gender, which may or may not correspond with the sex assigned at birth, including the personal sense of the body (which may involve, if freely chosen, modification of bodily appearance or function by medical, surgical, or other means) and other expressions of gender, including dress, speech and mannerisms.

(Yogyakarta Principles 2007: 6)

The queer academic in me responds immediately in noting that "sex" and "gender" are confused in the first definition and the rhetoric of "depth" in the second may or may not capture everyone's gender affiliations. Nevertheless, the document's attempt to negotiate the terrain of global diversity in its careful terminology is commendable, if the reader makes the always necessary Gadamerian move of trying to understand the complexities of the situation in which the speaker/writer operated and to appreciate the underlying motivational and utopian vision: "The Yogyakarta Principles [...] promise a different future where all people born free and equal in dignity and rights can fulfill that precious birthright" (2007: 7)

The Yogyakarta Principles accept the inevitability of global flows of knowledge, power, and legal border-crossings, while attempting to affirm the diversity that will also always characterize individuals' self-understanding in the context of a home culture, language, religion, nation, and region. Thus the Principles affirm the power and force of traditional beliefs ("Many States and societies impose gender and sexual orientation norms on individuals through custom, law and violence and seek to control how they experience personal relationships and how they identify themselves" [2007: 6]), even as it calls them into question by locating desired agency elsewhere: "Each person's self-defined sexual orientation and gender identity is integral to their personality and is one of the most basic aspects of self-determination, dignity, and freedom" (2007: 11). Any language indicating a judgment concerning "back-wardness" or "progress" is absent here; what the document foregrounds instead is the desired interplay between individual identity and norm, prejudice, and tradition. This locates the responsibility for definition not in the state, the church, or even the international human-rights body, but in the individual who may adopt, question, modify, or reject external impositions of identity, and who is vested with the "right" to do so in a way that overrides others' rights to impose.

Even so, the Yogyakarta Principles as a human-rights intervention cannot avoid impositional moves of its own. In stating as its first prin-ciple "The Right to the Universal Enjoyment of Human Rights" and adding as an explicit recommendation that states shall "Undertake pro-grams of education and awareness to promote and enhance the full enjoyment of human rights by all persons, irrespective of sexual orien-tation or gender identity" (2007: 10), the document is both participating in and calling for a top-down move by governments to reeducate (some would even say indoctrinate) citizens to become more tolerant of others. Not only is the practicality of this questionable but it also violates a principle of diversity in interlocution. Nowhere does the document indi-cate that its proponents' stances could be shaped and complicated by the variant beliefs of others; it is the intolerant other who must be changed. While I would never suggest that one can affirm the right to sexual identity and affirm the right to murder someone because of her/his sexual identity, I do believe that the exchange of information and perspective must be multilateral if one wishes to avoid the potential for destructiveness that always attends a posture of dogmatic self-satisfaction.

While the document speaks occasionally of "awareness-raising" (Yogyakarta Principles 2007: 13) and the like, it always assumes the position of the already meta-aware observer and judge. Principle 19 affirms "The Right to Freedom of Opinion and Expression," yet its recommendations affirm only the state's responsibility to change the opinions and expressions of those who dissent from the Yogyakarta Principles (2007: 24). This may be an unavoidable rhetorical move for a manifesto-like document, but the suppleness of another principle serves as a model. Principle 26 affirms "The Right to Participate in Cultural Life" and recommends that states "Foster dialogue between, and mutual respect among, proponents of the various cultural groups present within the State, including among groups that hold different views on matters of sexual orientation and gender identity, consistently with respect for the human rights referred to in these Principles" (Yogyakarta Principles 2007: 29). At the very least indicated therein is the sexual nonconformist's and the human-rights worker's responsibility to listen carefully as well as to assert forcefully. Granted, the frame is still one in which sexual/gender orientational rights trump all other rights, but at least dialogue is affirmed as a core mechanism for cultural change and understanding. Sometimes dialogue is not only the least we can hope for but also the best principle to affirm.

Perhaps the trickiest part of any document like the Yogyakarta Principles is enforcement, and that is certainly the case at hand. Its final principle is "Accountability": "Everyone whose human rights, including rights addressed in these Principles, are violated is entitled to have those directly or indirectly responsible for the violation, whether they are government officials or not, held accountable for their actions in a manner that is proportionate to the seriousness of the violation" (Yogyakarta Principles 2007: 31). Its recommendations include the establishment of "effective criminal, civil, administrative and other procedures" for bringing to justice all violators of human rights, and the creation of other unnamed "procedures" for the "enforcement of laws and policies" commensurate with the Yogyakarta Principles. There is no mention of any limits placed on such procedures or interventions, nor is there any mention of dialogue with states or other entities on how best to enforce the principles. While the document again follows the rhetorical pattern of manifestos here, the unilateralism of its enforcement-related recommendations makes me pause. Should the UN or the USA have intervened militarily to prevent or halt the genocide in Rwanda in 1994? Does an outside "power" parachute in, march in, or bomb selectively when moral or legal suasion fails? I was horrified at the Rwandan genocide during which many of my former colleagues at the national university were butchered by their fellow citizens. Theory reaches its limits at that point. When talking does nothing to halt murder, what comes next?

The Yogyakarta Principles clearly come down on the side of unnamed "procedures" that do not foreclose military options. While it may seem unlikely that any one nation will invade another to protect the right to sexual diversity, the rhetorical buildup to the US invasion of Afghanistan in 2001 included a laundry list of Taliban atrocities (including those against women) that masked Bush administration imperial designs in a cloak of human-rights rhetoric. Jasbir Puar worries rightly that uninterrogated notions of transnational queer rights can collude with "nationalist foreign policy [and embody] a tacit acceptance of U.S. imperialist expansion" (2005: 123). I am of a very mixed mind about when and how a nation or entity should ever halt forcefully the actions of another nation or entity, though I am not unsympathetic to the difficulties faced by any group attempting to craft a document like the Yogyakarta Principles. Perhaps the best that can happen is to use such a manifesto as a starting point for a conversation that tests its applicability through a widely ranging imagining of various concrete scenarios and possible responses. The Yogyakarta Principles are not the final word on the application of human-rights law to sexual and gender diversity, they are a preliminary articulation that will allow us to converse on any number of nuanced situations and challenges.

Those conversations are ongoing as I write this. In November 2007, the governments of Brazil, Argentina, and Uruguay, along with various NGOs, participated in the New York launch of the Principles as part of a campaign to gain UN consultative status for ABGLT (The Brazilian Gay, Lesbian, Bisexual and Trans Association). The Principles were translated into Nepalese and launched in Nepal in August of 2007 and were presented as part of a successful court case that lead to a Nepalese Supreme Court ruling in December 2007 mandating equal protection for all sexual minorities in the country. Needless to say, the conversation also involves those who are horrified by the possibilities represented in the document. Family Watch International, a conservative opponent of any recognition of the rights of non-heterosexuals, released a "Family Policy Brief" in 2007 that immediately picked up on the language of the

Yogyakarta Principles indicating (in their words) "Government Mandated Indoctrination and Thought Control" and the trampling on "Freedom of Speech" when contrary to the principles themselves. While the overall hyperbole and many outright lies of the Family Watch policy statement are inexcusable ("Even things like Mother's Day could be targeted"), we at least have to be conscious of the ways in which the rhetoric of documents such as the Yogyakarta Principles might allow and invite such responses because of unilateral statements. We always have to let the words of our interlocutors unsettle our self-assured stances. The conversation on "freedom," "rights," and sexual/gender diversity cannot only include those whose opinions are close to our own. We too have to be willing to listen and learn. Anything less that an eager willingness to engage in those difficult conversations is open to charges of an imperial trampling on the rights of others to disagree with us.

The future of the world ...

The ellipses in this concluding section title mark the unknowable and open-ended nature of global conversations on sexual diversity. While the Yogyakarta Principles imagine a telos of respect and legal protection, that is clearly a motivational utopia without immediate possibilities for realization. Gender and sexual nonconformists are attacked, killed, defamed, and denied housing and employment worldwide. The hatred and persecution of nonconformists does not mark a First World/Third World divide, and any discussion of progress on "queer rights" has to beware of the self-congratulation that urban queers in America or Europe often encode in their language and attitudes. I've been slurred and threatened with violence more often in New York and Los Angeles than I have anywhere else in the nation or the world. Self-questioning and the disruption of self-satisfaction are keys to the dialogic process if interlocutors want to accomplish anything other than further barricading themselves within their own horizons. Practically, this mandates saying "I was wrong" or "I was ill informed" and then learning from those mistakes.

It is a common move in Anglo-American works on globalization and sexuality studies to authorize oneself through an anecdote proving one's cosmopolitanism and respect for diverse cultures. In a way, I have already made such moves in talking about my visit to Tunisia and, previously, my Peace Corps experience, though what I have tried to emphasize in discussing both journeys were the learning opportunities they offered and lessons I still have to remind myself of often, even through this writing. However, I have hesitated to mention here any actual sexual experiences

I have had abroad because that topic is a minefield of possible over-generalizations and insensitivities. But then again without such revealing articulations we never expose ourselves in ways that lead to greater understanding and continued learning. I have never been shy about revealing my own stupidity.

My Peace Corps stint in Rwanda was rich in life experience but sexually barren. Rwanda, a Catholic and conservative nation, did not have a sexual subculture of same-sex desiring men that I ever located or was privy to, and the ex-pat community of Canadians, Belgians, and a few Americans was equally heterosexual or otherwise uninteresting or unavailable. I was twenty-four years old, lonely, and horny.

A summer 1985 trip to Kenya provided me the opportunity to visit much larger cities than any we had in Rwanda, to meet up with a friend who had traveled from the USA for a vacation, and generally to relax for a few weeks. It also offered me ample opportunities to act the fool. Walking out one evening from my Nairobi hotel, I noticed a Kenyan guy smiling at me. I returned the smile, he took my arm in a comradely way, and we walked together back to my hotel room. There he promptly robbed me and threatened to turn me in to the local police for criminal solicitation. He was nice enough to leave me my passport, though he took most of my money and left me with the wise advice to not be so foolish in the future as to think that any African man who looked my way was eager to jump into bed with a white man. "You fucked us as a colony, why would we want you to fuck us again?" I'll never forget that line. I swore off sex while in Africa.

Two weeks later, I was in the bar of a beach hotel in Malindi, north of Mombassa, playing cards with my American friend Bob, when I noticed a local guy staring at me from across the room. "Oh no," I thought to myself, "I'm not making that mistake again." But when I looked back, he was still smiling and then pointed down to the front of his pants which were tented out with an erection. As I said, I was lonely and horny ... so much for celibacy resolutions. I walked out to the nearby swimming pool and took a seat; he followed, and we started talking. He asked me why I was so shy given that we both knew we wanted sex with each other. I told him about my previous experience, which he was shocked by and attributed to the machinations of "a corrupt Nairobi whore from a bad family." He explained he wasn't going to rob me, he had borrowed his father's car to drive to the bar just "to get sex," and only wanted that and some friendly conversation. We both ended up having a good time with each other, talked for several hours, and stayed in touch for a couple of years through occasional letters. As the AIDS crisis and atten-dant wave of homophobic rhetoric shifted the discursive terrain in Kenya and beyond (as Mburu traces well in the essay mentioned earlier), he stopped writing. Some discrete conversations flourish for a while but then falter as people, needs, and contexts change, even as the conversation across cultures and sexual epistemologies inevitably continues.

My point in relating this story is simple. I had traveled abroad extensively by the time I spent my few weeks in Kenya, yet "read" the first encounter erroneously and then promptly "read" the second encounter erroneously as well. In both cases, my silent objectification of the others involved led to a failed hermeneutic experience. That is, until conversation began. While not all sexual encounters will be bracketed with strictly verbal exchanges (as I will explore in the second half of my next chapter), all must involve some form of sensitive and effective communication. This is hard enough to accomplish in a sex club in Los Angeles with regular clubgoers, much less in an international context where language and cultural differences magnify exponentially the possibility of miscommunication.

This is not to call for more or different cross-cultural sexual liaisons or to privilege sexual interactions over other interactions. It is to say, however, that the same best practices of listening and self-questioning pertain as much to the realm of sexuality as they do to other realms. It would be easy to dismiss sexuality as "just sex," but obviously sex is imbricated in networks of class, race, gender, cultural, and national power. Reading sexuality across cultures and languages offers possibilities for reading one's own position in a global conversation on privilege and ascribed intentions. It is one of the most lively, consequential, and power-fraught conversations imaginable. To speak to the other and listen to the other means, in obvious but often forgotten ways, that we become a little less stupid ourselves.

5   Radical sexuality and ethical responsibility

This book's queer conversation on the past, present, and future of sexuality studies is necessarily both transmedial and transhistorical. Voices from pop culture, high theory, and activism, as well as the near and distant past, all demand our respectful attention. A queer temporality and dialogic practice should not look for neat distinctions and linear progressions but, rather, for overlaps and dissonances that defy easy diachronic and synchronic compartmentalization. In some ways, queer studies admits the latter more regularly than the former. We attend to expressions emanating from television shows and films even more readily than to the voices of anyone from queer theory's past who seems a little stale or past her trendiness. Yet voices from one year, ten years, twenty years, and a century or more ago all urge themselves upon us as still relevant if always contextually imbricated. The 1970s, 1980s, or 1990s may seem long ago and long superseded to some, but the narrative of quick change animating such a mindset is itself a reflection of a Nietzschean and Foucauldian theoretical framework that warrants critical attention, as I have suggested throughout this book. Gadamer urges us to be wary of the arrogance of the present, which treats interlocutors from yesteryear as quaint and warranting only a cursory nod from a position of self-congratulatory superiority. He asks us to listen more humbly.

We still have much to learn from our queer foremothers and forefathers. As I noted earlier, over a quarter century after its first appearance in 1984, Gayle Rubin's "Thinking Sex" continues to help us confront and understand the ongoing American obsession with a "domino theory of sexual peril," with its rigid wall demarcating the "normal, natural, healthy, holy" from the "abnormal, unnatural, sick, sinful" (Rubin 1993: 14). American moral and religious anxiety still fixates on that barricade, the line "between sexual order and chaos," for the fear is that "if anything is permitted to cross this erotic DMZ [demilitarized zone], the barrier against scary sex will crumble and something unspeakable will skitter across" (Rubin 1993: 14). Rubin, writing less than a decade after the conclusion of the Vietnam War and the thorough discrediting of the Nixonian domino theory of Southeast Asian political peril, repudiates the wall metaphor, calling instead for a "pluralistic sexual ethics" that would

> judge sexual acts by the way partners treat one another, the level of mutual consideration, the presence or absence of coercion, and the quantity and quality of the pleasure they provide. Whether sex acts are gay or straight, coupled or in groups, naked or in underwear, commercial or free, with or without video, should not be ethical concerns.
>
> (Rubin 1993: 15)

In her Butler-anticipating attempt to dismantle the reigning architecture of our sexual identity politics, Rubin offers us still a usefully different configuration of a sexual/ethical system, theorized as one of benign sexual variation in a context of respect and consent.

Rubin's is a provocative and therefore especially useful voice in the classroom because she is so forthrightly idealistic in her hopes for a thorough overhaul of our sexual order. Yet as motivational as her articulations are, the devil is always in the details, so to speak. "Twenty years or so" did not lead to radical social change. Any new sexual praxis would necessarily rely on mundane and often mechanical, unreflective decisions, and would depend also upon successful struggles with bodies/ desires/prejudices/reactions that are neither predictable nor instrumentally controllable, tied as they are to the incremental processes by which we impact and alter our contexts even as those changing contexts work dialogically on and with us. While I concur with Rubin in her use of "mutual consideration" as the centerpiece of a new sexual ethics of benign variation, my hermeneutic interests lead me also always to consider how such mutuality will always be compromised and often only imperfectly achieved. Rubin is brash, some even say rash, in her embrace of intergenerational desire, commercial sex, and incestuous desire as part of that benign variation, ignoring the fact that mutuality is especially complex, suspect, and contestable when one factors in the differential power relationships of age, economics, and familial dynamics. These complications are where our conversation must linger if we are to move beyond manifesto and embrace lived practice in its ethical ambiguity, as I would have us do in this chapter.

Needless to say, it is difficult to imagine or credibly theorize a perfectly level field for human interaction, unless posited as a bland homogeneity that would likely kill all forms of desire. Alan Sinfield has termed the lip-service given full "similarity and equality" in gay relationships an "egalitarian ideology" that is dishonest and unrealistic (2004: 59–63). I would see a coupling based on a perfect sameness of location within all matrixes of power and knowledge as an interactional version of the mirror-gazing that doomed David of *Giovanni's Room* to epistemological stasis. Even as an ideal, that figuration is far too "homo" for my tastes. This book has argued repeatedly that all learning—whether self or other directed, whether sexual, social, or something else entirely—depends necessarily upon difference. Yet with differences come responsibilities as intense as the desires that they often generate.

For sex radicals on a quest to test/probe/learn, our fundamental hetero-sexuality demands an equally heterogeneous conversational practice whereby we grapple with the lived ethical difficulties of responding to difference in our process of sexual exploration. Given the inevitable tensions between the desire to question/transgress the norms of sexual propriety and the ongoing ethical demand for consent and respect, the best that we can do is to linger in gray areas where failures and successes are murky and debatable. It would be too easy to focus in a discussion of "radical sexual ethics" on erotic pairings of S&M enthusiasts or fetishists with their elaborate system of safe words and nonverbal, but well-codified, signals of request and consent. Manuals such as Jay Wiseman's *SM 101* (now in its second edition) make some forms of fetish play as easy to learn and navigate as PowerPoint or Excel. Much harder are those liaisons where desire for transgression and exploration takes one into encounters where communication is imprecise and consent is questionable because of significant complications—linguistic, economic, or even through level of impairment resulting from drug or alcohol use. Those cases put our Gadamerian practices to the test.

In the coming pages, I will examine two texts—one print and the other personal. In juxtaposing the late Victorian erotic memoir *My Secret Life* with my own wanderings through the sexual subculture of Los Angeles a century later, I can hardly provide anything more than instances that exemplify or call into question the utility of the theory base that I am exploring throughout this book. They capture, imperfectly and idiosyncratically, the general complexity of living ethically as a sexual radical. Yet these are the very problem-riddled narratives that we must offer to each other more frequently and discuss more thoroughly if theory is ever to become praxis. Praxis is the mundane, the imperfect, and the always individually adapted, as theoretical generalizations and broad narrative patterns encounter the complications of the personal context, the unique life history, and the individual body in all of its peculiarities. Walter's story from *My Secret Life* and my story from Los Angeles are only useful as points of conversational contact and reflection. Yet those points are crucial for the dialogical process of knowledge generation and personal/political transformation. As we read others critically yet generously we can be (if we allow ourselves to be) better positioned to read ourselves modestly yet creatively.

Body fluid desire

The autobiographical narrative *My Secret Life* demands such critical generosity. It speaks to us out of a subject position that is at once eccentric and culturally embedded. First published around the turn of the twentieth century, *My Secret Life* traces one man's sexual musings and obsessions while revealing a stunning array of prejudices concerning gender, race, class, marriage, child-rearing, and education. It confronts us with at least two Gadamerian challenges. One arises from the tension between the power of prejudice/tradition and the radical, transformative power of critique. The other derives from the confrontation between the individual ego of the solipsist (however traditional or radical she or he might be) and the perspectives and demands of those individuals surrounding the solipsist whose varying needs and voices warrant attention and consideration. By examining that tension and confrontation, we— well over a century later—can begin to outline a theory and practice of an ethics of sex radicalism, by learning what we can from our predecessors' successes, trials, and errors. Hermeneutic theory challenges us always to test ourselves against what we read and to fuse with and try on a text's narratives as possibilities for our own always changing life plan. As we read, respond to, and at times resist its narrative, *My Secret Life* insists that we confront directly the fact or fiction of a "domino theory of sexual peril," and the potential for chaos to result from a wholesale rejection of the "normal." Its horizon tests and challenges ours as it makes for an intense and unsettling reading experience.

My Secret Life offers a reading experience of a reading experience—a hermeneutic bonanza of sorts. What makes it particularly pertinent here is its narrator's propensity to read the norms of his own era and his own incorporation of those norms, which he challenges with startling frankness and ingenuity as he seeks to put into practice a radical, neolibertine sexual philosophy. Walter repeatedly asks variants of the following questions:

> Why may a man and a woman handle each other's privates, and yet it be wrong for a man to feel another's prick, or a woman to feel

another's cunt? Every one in each sex has at one period of their lives done so, and why should not any society of association of people indulge in these innocent, tho sensual, amusements if they like in private? What is there in their doing so that is disgraceful? It is prejudice of education alone which teaches it is.

(Kincaid 1996: 248)

In musing this way, Walter performs the skeptical hermeneutic inquiry that Gadamer calls for—questioning prejudice and attempting to sort out prejudice's effects. His bodily failure at times to "put into practice" what he believes allows for sustained reflection in the text on the power of "prejudice" to determine even our physical responses. We see this most memorably in an early scene of attempted anal sex with another man, whom he meets through his companion Betsy.

"Put it up me."—he said.—"I can't, my prick won't stand." [...] I turned sick, but after a time I turned his arse towards me, and got my prick stiff by hard frigging, determined to try what buggery was like. But the moment I put it against his arsehole down it drooped [...] tho I tried again and again, determined to know everything, and to do everything once in my life, it was useless.

(Kincaid 1996: 285)

Walter later ruminates,

my curiosity seemed unsatisfied and I had a sort of desire to learn more, yet a dislike to myself for desiring it.—When she asked me if she should get him again, I refused point blank, yet all the time longing to try, and dissatisfied at not having put my prick up him, to see if it gave some unknown pleasure or not.

(Kincaid 1996: 286)

We cannot "will to desire," as I explored in my first chapter; indeed, here we find a will to learn that confronts the synchronic limits on sexual desire. A century and a half before the Deep Springers discovered that they could not put their queer theory into queer bodily practice, Walter runs up against the same limits on praxis.

Walter, unlike the Deep Springers, did not give up easily. What Gadamerian theory reminds us is that a synchronic limit is not a diachronic one, which *My Secret Life* well demonstrates. While Walter's body fails him time and again as he attempts to break powerful taboos against sex with other men, he pushes the limits of his own sexual responsiveness with resilience and significant, though incremental, success. After the elapse of some years, he mentions to his then companion Sarah that he would like "to feel a man's prick, to see closely his prick standing, see his spunk come out much or little" (Kincaid 1996: 387). What follows, he describes as "the crowning act of my eroticism, the most daring fact of my secret life" (Kincaid 1996: 386). Having Sarah procure a young, heterosexual working man, desperately in need of money ("without employment for two months" [Kincaid 1996: 387]), Walter engages in a lengthy attempt to resist thoroughly "early teaching and prejudices" (1996: 387) and push his sexual responses into new arenas. I'll leave aside the class components of this exchange for the moment (returning to them below) to note simply that the young man is compliant in being paid for his sexual services, and though "fear and shame" (Kincaid 1996: 390) continually plague Walter's responses, he perseveres instead of immediately sending the man away. While at first the young man (who has had no previous experience with or interest in other men) also does not respond to Walter's attempt to stimulate him, Walter finally succeeds by bringing Sarah into the room. He is able to arouse the young man by masturbating him while he looks at Sarah and to achieve the goal of seeing another man ejaculate. Walter too is aroused enough to have sex with Sarah using the other man's semen as lubricant.

If the scenario ended there, it would be an interesting exercise in manipulating contexts to allow one to achieve a philosophical goal related to sexuality (to challenge what we today would term the regulatory regime of "hetero/homo," still manifested in the narrative as "non-sodomite/sodomite") in spite of one's lack of specifically sexual desire. Such would be a Victorian instance of using an external prop (today, Viagra and some porn) to help one make a theoretically supported but otherwise physically resisted point. However, desires, themselves, prove surprisingly, incrementally flexible here:

> Next morning at breakfast I thought, "That debauch will never be renewed." After luncheon, "What was the harm after all." Then I began to think I should like to feel him once more, to watch the phenomenon of the spend more coolly and philosophically. [...] It is a chance which never may come again to me.
>
> (Kincaid 1996: 403)

Having Sarah bring him around for several more sessions, Walter soon begins to notice a change in himself: "Before when feeling his prick it did not make me randy—tonight it did" (Kincaid 1996: 404). Walter fellates him, fondles him often, and, with growing interest, begins to comment on his attractiveness. As Walter continues his experimentations with the young man, Sarah's presence becomes unnecessary for the two of them to achieve orgasm with each other:

> My baudy imagination being set to work, all sorts of possibilities came into my head. We soaped well our pricks, and under our balls and ass furrow. They lying on the top of him, we thrust our pricks under each other's balls, and working in the soapy furrows, both spent on each other's backside.
>
> (Kincaid 1996: 405)

The young man responds also with increasing desire, meeting Walter alone and saying, "When I thought of it all, I got to want it" (Kincaid 1996: 404). Walter's reading of this: "Novelty stimulates desire" (Kincaid 1996: 405). He notes that "These lascivious vagaries and delicacies did not suggest themselves all at once" (Kincaid 1996: 406), they occur to him gradually over time as his desires shift in concert with the changing responses of the young man himself. He concludes: "My libidinosity increased by indulging it" (Kincaid 1996: 407). Neat compartments of gender-based desire abrade over time, and while a falling domino does not capture the dynamic of change here, a sexual wall certainly loses a few stones because of growing familiarity and the discovery of pleasurable sensations of flesh on flesh, no matter the gender.

Conversation also weathers that wall. Talking, projecting forward, and even group brainstorming are all key to the increasingly diverse amusements of Walter, the young man, and Sarah: "The conversation was always erotic. [...] Behold us soon all three on the bed, she with his prick in her mouth and he with my prick in his mouth. I feeling about her cunt and his balls, as well as the difficult attitude permitted" (Kincaid 1996: 408–9). Though Walter repeatedly states that he is disgusted by the thought of anal sex with the young man, when Sarah suggests it, he tries it again, with success, and with both men reaching orgasm in the act. In good Gadamerian fashion, they challenge and teach each other as the conversational dynamic diversifies and intensifies their repertoire of erotic practices.

Yet *My Secret Life* also reveals the limits on conversational instrumentality; Walter's diversions and successes do not lead necessarily to permanent alterations in his sexual selfhood. Afterwards he remembers the act of anal sex "with disgust," though he notes also that "it is against [his] philosophy even to think [he] had done wrong" (Kincaid 1996: 417). Tradition in the form of sedimented sexual desires retain their force. However malleable sexuality may prove as contexts and conversations change, one's sexual desire cannot be appropriately figured as a falling domino, as a switch that turns on or off (well evidenced still in that fact that homosexual activity in prisons does not lead to sustained homosexual relationships outside of prison). Having pushed his boundaries successfully—achieved his praxis-based goals—Walter sends the young man away (as abruptly and even callously as he acted when he first procured him) and returns to a sexual life centered mostly on women.

The above scenes compel us to reflect on the temporality of desire, how desire is malleable over time and how context and opportunity can lead to shifts, expansions, and contractions, even if temporary. While we cannot "will to desire" in instrumental fashion, desires are not static; they are fully imbricated within our changing environment, over which we do have some measure of influence or control. *My Secret Life* offers us something of a phenomenology of morphic desire as it describes in rich detail Walter's processing of the new sensations generated by slippery bodies and welcoming orifices, one that prefigures the final orgiastic swimming-pool scene in *The Rocky Horror Picture Show,* where the formerly heterosexual Brad and Janet are caught up in a dynamic of giving themselves over to "absolute pleasure" with each other, Rocky, and the Walter-like Doctor Frank-N-Furter. Having worked to disconnect sensual pleasure from reigning systems of moral valuation, Walter invites us to join him in the swimming pool, at least for a quick dip. Some may politely decline, but, as I speculated in my introduction, few people would choose *not* to eat at the banquet of life if given a free meal ticket. That is the first hermeneutic opportunity afforded by *My Secret Life.*

Yet many other reading challenges present themselves as well. At his most intellectually and personally daring (because, in Gadamerian fashion, self-questioning and vulnerable), Walter pursues his self-described "philosophy" of sexual rebellion in active discussion with others, including one long-term companion Camille. He writes,

> Why is it abominable for any one to look at man and woman fucking [...] ? Is copulation an improper thing, if not, why is it disgraceful to look at is being done? [...] Such reflexions for some years had crossed my mind; they tended to sweep away prejudices. [...] In these opinions I was strengthened by repeated conversations with Camille. She [...] had a wonderful cool common sense way of looking at things. When I had doubts about the propriety of doing this or that, she would solve them with answers which appeared to me irrefutable, at length. We seem to have been on the subject of unusual pleasures whenever we met.—In fact we were constantly talking about varieties in lustful enjoyments. She would sit down

smoking a cigarette, and I a cigar, and consider whether there was wrong in frigging, gamahuching, minetting, tribadism, or sodomy.— In men frigging each other, or women doing the same, and other things. Our conclusion was that there was no harm in any of them.

(Kincaid 1996: 248–9)

He is similarly loquacious with Betsy, Sarah, and several other partners who join him in an intense, micro-communal questioning and abrasion of Victorian sexual norms. *My Secret Life* reveals well the many attitudes, motivations, and enthusiasms (as well as skepticisms and hesitations) within this small group of Victorian sexual adventurers and sex workers.

However, the pernicious power and inherent violence of Victorian prejudices is also memorably revealed in the text, as sexuality becomes the nodal point where norms regarding childrearing, race, class, and gender meet. From an early age, Walter is exposed to the worst myths of Victorian pseudo-sexology, repeatedly being told by his godfather that masturbation leads to tragedy: "You look ill [...] you've been frigging yourself [...] I can see it in your face, you'll die in a mad-house, or of consumption" (Kincaid 1996: 59). Walter tells us, "He repeated this so often that it sunk deeply into my mind, and made me uneasy" (Kincaid 1996: 35). Walter is open and vulnerable here in a conversational encounter, though this is far from the Gadamerian ideal of chosen epistemological vulnerability. It is instead an abuse of vulnerability through an inculcation of fear and self-loathing.

Walter is acculturated, early on and in multiple ways, into an inter-actional dynamic of abuse. He tells us that his first memory is of being repeatedly sexually molested by a housemaid when he is somewhere between the "age of five and eight years" (Kincaid 1996: 23). He later hears his mother mention that "When Walter was a little fellow, she had dismissed a filthy creature, whom she had detected in abominable practices with one of her children" (Kincaid 1996: 24–5). Abominable they are, but even if Walter repeats that word in his own recounting, Walter the oft-abused becomes Walter the active abuser when he becomes a sexual being, and finds ample cultural/ideological support for his deployment of power over others, whether pecuniary (as indicated above) or physical as we also see repeatedly.

Walter is scripted into reigning economic and gender power structures. First, his older cousin Fred (whom he describes as "a very devil from his cradle" [Kincaid 1996: 31]) repeatedly mocks his timidity and insecurity, urging him to treat servants and the working class with contempt, and then manipulating him (at age twelve) into peeping at and sexually fondling his sleeping younger sister. These lessons are then redoubled by another "older friend" who forcefully imprints on Walter the exact process by which Victorian young men should "seduce" women:

> Tell her you have seen her cunt, and make a snatch up her petticoats when no one is near; keep at it, and you will be sure to get a feel, and some day, pull out your prick, say straight you want to fuck her, girls like to see a prick, she will look, even if she turns her head away. This advice he dinned into my ears continually.
>
> (Kincaid 1996: 67)

At this crucial point in the formation of his sexual horizon, there are no counter-balancing voices urging restraint, except that of his godfather who speaks only about continence and celibacy until marriage. It is a tragic conversational void.

In his initial attempt to put his friend's words into action, Walter accosts Charlotte, one of his family's housemaids, whom he first verbally harasses, "then she began to cry. Just as I was begging pardon, my friend's advice again rang in my ears, I stooped and swiftly ran both hands up her clothes" (Kincaid 1996: 67). In repeated acts of increasingly aggressive sexual assault, he continuously hears his friend's voice: "'Snatch at her cunt,' rang in my ears" and then "My friend's advice came again to me: pushing my right hand still between her thighs, with my left I pulled out my prick, as stiff as a poker" (Kincaid 1996: 69). Backed by gender and class Victorian ideologies epitomized in the voice of his older friend, Walter discounts the voice of the woman pleading with him, and, with his friend's voice continuing to ring in his ears, he commits his first act of rape. While he discovers various interlocutors who help him challenge Victorian sexual norms, he never attends to or values the few (female, pleading) voices that challenge the class- and gender-based components of his worldview. Gender and class hierarchies are thoroughly naturalized in the text, even if sexual norms are successfully denaturalized.

However much potential Walter has, and it is considerable, as an incisive reader of Victorian sexual discourse, he is no exemplar of Gadamerian inquiry. The worst implication of a hermeneutic approach to human interaction and other human beings is the possibility of violent, uni-directional objectification. And that is exactly what Walter is repeatedly guilty of, and in sometimes horrific ways. As we have seen, he is most at ease when paying individuals for sex, in effect, owning their bodies for contracted periods of time. His treatment of children in this way is especially appalling, as he matter-of-factly describes several acts of procurement and rape of young girls. Similarly, on a trip to France, he pays to watch two "Negroes" have sex and then attempts sex with a woman of African heritage; he describes the acts and the individuals involved in the most dehumanizing and racist terms. In these and innumerable other scenes, he "reads" others without letting them challenge any of his own prejudices. He is a miserably failed hermeneut. If Walter had been willing or able to allow interlocutors to challenge him on ideological constructs beyond those of sexuality, he could have been a revolutionary thinker advancing an early form of social constructionism, offered as a critical approach to all forms of prejudice and tradition. He certainly has the requisite inquisitiveness and intellectual flexibility to do so.

Such was not the case, and Walter's insensitivity has led to many harsh readerly responses, from Stephen Marcus's early characterization of it as showing us "as nothing else I know does, the pathos of perversity, how deeply sad, how cheerless a condemnation it really is" (1964: 127), to outrage from my students every semester I teach it, some of whom brand the text as wholly revolting and Walter as simply psychopathic. Outrage is not analysis, of course, as fully justified as outrage is in cases of rape, gross misuse of power, and physical or emotional violence. *My Secret Life* compels the sexually radical, ethically responsible reader to sort out Walter's grossest mistakes from his laudably rebellious actions, his unforgivably violent usage of others from his commendably determined reactions to the violent strictures of his culture. Walter fails ethically because he does not listen when others disagree with him; his early decision to tune out the impositions of Victorian pseudo-sexology—epitomized in the warnings of his godfather—means that he also tunes out everyone who attempts to check his quest for probing the limits of his own sexual responsiveness. He lives the Gadamerian injunction to engage sexual prejudice and discover new truths through a method of skeptical hermeneutic inquiry. However, he wholly ignores the Gadamerian call to ethics through self-displacement and a conversational disruption of the solipsism that can accompany vigorous critical engagement. To paraphrase Ricoeur, he seeks his own "good life," but not one "with and for others, in just institutions."

While a superficial reading of the text might support a "domino theory" of perversion, with Walter's sexual experimentation leading inevitably to rape, abuse, and moral chaos, that judgment would mistake the symptom for the cause. Walter does not act monstrously because he transgresses Victorian sexual norms; the monstrosity of those norms elicits strategies of critical response that are themselves caught up in a broad culture and physics of abuse. Walter challenges his own limits and those of his era, and in doing so, is unwavering and unresponsive to the needs of others. Walter's crimes against the humanity of others are horrifying, but unless we attempt to understand the complex origins of his troubled and troubling worldview, we too fail as ethically engaged hermeneuts.

I would rather let Walter's own words challenge our categories, much as he finds ways to contest the very language and categories of his culture:

> Many who have not tasted our sexual pleasures will call them beastly. They are not. But what if they are?—What are all physical functions of man and woman, what is chewing, drinking, spitting, snotting, urinating, farting?—What is copulation? Is that beastly?—Certainly it is what beasts do.—They will call that natural perhaps, but it's a purely animal act, tho not specially beastly to me. [...] What is the joining of tongues, the mixing of salivas, the gluing of two mouths together when fucking?—beastly? But there's no harm in these it will be said, it's natural.—Be it so.—So are other erotic amusements equally natural and not more beastly.—What more harm in a man licking a woman's clitoris to give her pleasure, or of she sucking his cock for the same purpose, both taking pleasure in giving each other pleasure. So if a man plugs a woman's bum-hole with his finger when they are copulating or gamahuching, and so with other sensual devices and fancies, they are all equally natural tho many may not enjoy them.—All are permissible if a couple do them for mutual delight, *and are no more beastly than simple human copulation*.
>
> (Kincaid 1996: 468)

If only, we might say, he had followed his own philosophical edicts and ensured that all he did was "for mutual delight" and was consensually performed. He did not and is culpable for that failure. As Rubin points out, sexual variation is a benign concept, whether that variation is synchronically or diachronically manifested; Walter's changing desires do not in and of themselves represent an ethical problem. He fails ethically because he ignores the requisite principle of consent. Young children, bought from a procurer, cannot consent. The women he raped did not consent. Whether we use Rubin's term—"mutual consideration"—or his—"mutual delight"—Walter's ethical failings are those of abysmally failed communication.

Sex club text

Walter's crimes against humanity provide a narrative trajectory that might give us cause for concern about the viability of a radical sexual ethics. Yet his failures contrast usefully with the successes of others who have lived ethically while also questioning the powerful strictures delineating the normal from the abnormal. I evoked Xaviera Hollander in my introduction to this book; she remains one of the great sexual adventurers of the twentieth century, one who retained a clear sense of interpersonal ethics while engaging in her norm-challenging pursuits. Equally memorable are Samuel Delany's recountings of his navigations through New York gay sexual subculture in *The Motion of Light in Water* (1988) and *Times Square Red, Times Square Blue* (1999). The latter book, in particular, is pertinent here because of the sophistication of its analysis regarding the changing landscape of the New York sex scene. Delany is a superb reader of the text of the porn theatre and the surrounding street life of hustlers and horny men. His overarching thesis is a basic but important one: That what transpires in porn theatres, sex clubs, and similar venues is deeply intertwined with broader culture, that (following Rubin) "public sex situations" (as he terms what is actually privately venued but still visible or semi-visible sex for those consenting to enter the venue) "are not Dionysian and uncontrolled but are rather some of the most highly socialized and conventionalized behavior human beings can take part in" (Delany 1999: 158). They are part of a continuum of benign sexual variation. Institutions such as "clubs, [...] baths, tea-room sex, gay porn movie houses [...] do not propagate insanely in some extrasocial and unconstrained 'outside/beyond,' apart from any concept of social responsibility—and that includes what goes on in the orgy rooms at the baths" (Delany 1999: 193–4). However much some politicians and moralizers may decry such institutions as indicating "the End of Civilization as We Know It," they "are always already within the social; indeed, they *are* the social—and are not outside it" (Delany 1999: 198). In detailing the often friendly and supportive, though occasionally crass and abusive, ways that men interact within sex venues, Delany makes the point that the text of the sex venue is simply a variation on the text of human being and community.

As *Reading Sexualities* has made clear, I agree, and certainly my timid venturings during the 1980s into the New York venues that Delany describes confirm the veracity of his descriptions of the ordinariness of the interactions, with the exception that sex was involved. I found conversation, camaraderie, both sensitivity and insensitivity, and the usual range of human behaviors and personalities, simply with sex added to the mix. To be sure, "simply" does not capture the complexity of the possible ramifications of sexual interaction when HIV transmission is a possibility and when visitors to sex venues bring with them preexisting and sometimes tortured perspectives on their own sexual identity and erotic desires and the potentially shameful nature of what they are doing at the venue. In a sense, there is nothing simple about it, yet that complexity does not mitigate ethical responsibility. Sexuality matters in the equation of what happens in a sex venue, but degrees of responsibility and irresponsibility, of honest and dishonest communication, and of openness to others and their needs or a selfish prioritization of one's own pleasures and comforts pertain, whatever the social situation. The ideals of openness, exchange, and interaction-based change are no more or less pertinent in a XXX zone than they are in a social gathering or classroom setting. Yet in some ways the unique intensities of the sex club allow us paradigmatic cases for discussions of interpersonal responsibility.

I focus here on two questions that sex clubs allow us to foreground: "What is consent?" and "Is objectification dependent upon a destructive dynamic of oppressor/oppressed?" Both take us beyond the ethical failings evident in *My Secret Life* and both touch on Gadamerian conceptions of openness, communication, and responsibility. My own ethnography of the sex club is drawn primarily from my experiences in two Los Angeles venues: "The Zone" and "Basic Plumbing," encompassing a dozen years starting in the early 1990s. While my stories are idiosyncratic, my point remains that all of life is to some extent. It is only through the juxtaposition and critical interplay of those idiosyncrasies (and discovery of overlaps) that we come to learn anything about ourselves or the world.

Consent is simultaneously a straightforward and highly complicated issue, one that leads Sinfield to note, "Where we consent, [...] we may be most deluded," though he adds "Not much can be done about this" (2004: 51). My own impulse is to probe that murkiness. In the case of a sex club, the payment of a membership fee and then entrance into a club demarcates a passing into a private space that represents one relatively straightforward form of consent. A sex club or bathhouse is a place where by entering one consents to see and be surrounded by a wide variety of sexual activities. One also, as one comes (usually quickly) to understand some of the fundamental rules of the club, consents to be sexually propositioned in a variety of subtle and not-so-subtle ways. One agrees to allow verbal solicitations, lascivious looks, and (where we begin to encounter considerable ambiguity) some forms of non-aggressive touch. A light, brushing touch anywhere on the body, including the genitals, is normally allowed so long as it is not heavy-handed and is posed as a question regarding the acceptability of further activity. A movement away or, more commonly, a light tap of the hand by the recipient of the touch—at the Zone, three taps indicating "thanks, I'm flattered, but no thanks"—ends the encounter. Or should. Los Angeles was always a complicated and exciting place because of the huge influx of visitors every summer. That made for an ever-changing population of new sex-club-goers and endless confusion. "Tourists," one guy said to me in a lounge area, "I love 'em, but I wish they would figure out the signals." He had been tapping gently at the arm of someone who was groping him with deepening enthusiasm and the other guy thought it was a welcoming movement. He finally had to push the guy away and say gruffly, "No!" No national or international code exists for such negotiations (as I have found out, on the other side of things, in some non-LA venues), which makes communication often a process of negotiation, trial, and error. "Reading" the others' attempts at communicating desire or lack thereof often becomes an exercise in interpretation as complicated as any act of literary interpretation or translation.

Over time, if one is a persistent club-goer in the same venue, one does learn its basic language and how to converse with some competence through a complex system of verbal and physical signs. At the Zone and other LA venues, on your knees, mouth slightly open, means you want to suck someone. Standing up, arms crossed, but legs spread, means "I am willing to let someone suck me." And so on. Other than the tourists who misread cues and persisted in their misreading until testily corrected, I have never found people to be anything other than polite and respectful of others' boundaries, once they were discovered. Though miscommunications are always occurring even among regulars, they are usually quickly forgotten and forgiven. Sex clubs are thus as orderly and as ethically charged as any other venue where people meet in high numbers, in constricted spaces, and interact: restaurants, dance clubs, Wal-Mart, football games. I've seen a few arguments between individuals who had a history or were talking about something non-sex-related, but mostly consent is given or denied and respected.

Yet that generalization begs several questions. The first has to do with one's ability to consent to harm oneself. I have had to confront my own prejudices on this topic. I have seen innumerable acts of bareback anal intercourse in sex clubs. I was horrified the first time I entered an orgy room and saw a young man getting fucked by five or six guys in succession, all without a condom. Given that I was a volunteer at that time with an HIV education and support organization, my first impulse was to jump in and lecture the guy about taking such foolish risks to his health. I knew it was highly improbable that I was witnessing a scene of sero-conversion—I had seen the same young man in the club many times—but even if he had long been HIV+, I well knew it was hardly a wise idea to have condomless sex with many strangers.

But I didn't intervene. I had to grapple with my own conceptualization of consent and personal freedom. No one was being coerced, everyone present was in their twenties or older (well into an age range where we commonly allow for the ability to consent), and there were already many pamphlets lying around that gave ample advice about safer and riskier forms of sex. We were handed free condoms when we entered the club. A conversation regarding sexual desires, personal boundaries, and comfort with risk was taking place already in that venue—my voice of moralizing would not have been appropriate or efficacious. After all, the moralizing voices of religious zealots and bigots, intruding into our conversations without invitation, are precisely what the radical sex community is already barraged by. However murky the internal dynamics of consent may be, however deluded we may feel others are in consenting, we must cede people their own authority to make choices about their bodily activities and parameters of comfort. As indicated in the previous chapter's discussion of reading other's lives scornfully and intervening internationally, I am very wary of judging others' decisions and modes of being, especially when no one is asking for our opinion. If we approach sexuality without the sense of exaggerated moral panic that Rubin condemns, then we would be no more likely to intervene or even comment audibly on an act of barebacking than we would in seeing an obese couple gorge themselves at a fast-food restaurant or an asthmatic smoke a cigarette on a park bench. It is none of our damned business.

In saying this, I clearly part ways from the call to common, communal action and perspective of Tim Dean (whose work I greatly admire). Building on the analysis of social ecologist Gabriel Rotello, Dean asserts that "gay men practicing unsafe sex are failing to act collectively in the interests of gay men as a group" (2000: 140–1), that a broad perspective on what is "good" for gay men should trump the individual's desires or comfort with risk. My perspective is that the "macro" (the community's needs) should always remain conversant with, but should not unilaterally determine the "micro" (the individual's needs and desires). I am not comfortable with any demand that members of a socially distinct and disadvantaged group act only in ways that uphold some desired image of healthy, self-loving, and poster-worthy community representatives. Nor do I accept his premise that "Unlike other risky behaviors such as smoking, drinking, and substance abuse [...] unsafe sex [uniquely] always directly involves somebody else" (Dean 2000: 140). The only thing that distinguishes unsafe sex from unsafe communal eating patterns or norms of tobacco use is that sex elicits from us an exaggerated response. Such continued overreaction to all things "sexual" may even play into a dynamic rendering unsafe sex especially taboo and therefore especially desirable, further undermining any effective discussion of risk and responsibility. Productive conversations about a wide variety of unhealthy practices—ranging from cultural patterns of morbid obesity and heart disease in rural America to drug use and risky sexual activity among some gay men—demand a much more matter-of-fact approach to desires for pleasure (food-, tobacco-, or sex-related) than is allowed by a continued overreading of the "meaning" of condomless sex by some gay men. Horny heterosexual young adults fuck without condoms all the time, and no one frets about some communal death-centered "ego-ideal" that they are evincing thereby, as Dean worries is the case for gay men (2000: 150). People consent to harm themselves often and in a myriad of ways, and take foolish risks with alarming frequency, something that we certainly should educate against but not find especially surprising or single out as revealing a unique characteristic of a given micro-community. My dad followed his own father in smoking himself into an early death by lung cancer despite first-hand evidence, his doctor's warnings, and years of high-profile antismoking campaigns; frankly, many of my students are following micro-communal patterns of tobacco use that will lead to a similar outcome. The best we can do is engage in nonhysterical conversations about pleasure, risk, and responsibility.

Of course, consent can be far murkier even than the above example indicates. Both in sex-club and in non-sex-club interactions, impairment has a significant impact on the ability to consent. I have seen innumerable people who were clearly inebriated or high in clubs, and no doubt their capacity to weigh risks and make considered decisions was heavily compromised. David Archard makes a pertinent point in his book *Sexual Consent*. He suggests that consensuality rests on three key principles: capacity, information, and voluntariness. Information bears on sex-club activity, obviously, in that one might conceivably lie about one's HIV status and participate in risky sex, endangering another person who believes he is not at risk. One cannot rely on another's honesty in an anonymous situation—hence the oft-stated rule to interact with everyone as if he is HIV+. Voluntariness also bears, as we have seen, in the way that one respects the other's right to say "no," though the other also has to respect one's right to ask or invite. I have never seen voluntariness seriously compromised. Anything other than hushed whispers in an area of the club designated for sex leads to the immediate attention of other patrons and security guards. Radical "public" sex is often remarkably well-policed sex.

Archard then spends some time discussing the nuances of "capacity" in a way that pertains here. He writes:

> Many people engage in drunken sex. It is true, but not telling, that individuals may, when drunk, have sex that they would not have when sober. For it is also true, and telling, that when sober, they know this to be the case and get drunk in that knowledge. [...] That

is, they "consent" to their drunkenness. Insofar as they do, their consent when drunk may be presumed valid. [...]

However, there is a further question. At what point of drunkenness may an individual's agreement to sex be considered beside the point? There must be such a point even if there was an initial willingness to start getting drunk. Somebody may agree to make themselves incapable of giving their consent. Such an achieved incapacity undercuts the validating force of the original first voluntary step. There is a continuum of drunkenness which runs from tipsy to comatose. Clearly a comatose person is not able to consent to (or even properly participate in) sexual activity. But, even short of being unconscious, somebody may be so drunk as not to be aware of what they are doing or incapable of making a decision.

(Archard 1998: 45)

Archard cannot name the precise point when one becomes incapable of giving consent; that is always one for the ethically committed potential partner to read and judge with care. Archard's only clear-cut reminders are that someone who did not consent to becoming inebriated (was slipped a drug or a doctored drink) would never have the capacity to consent to later activities, and that acts involving individuals grossly or involuntarily impaired are acts of rape.

Here again the ethics of the sex club are the ethics of everyday life: Consent cannot be given by any person without the capacity to consent. This would be true of taking money from someone who is drunk, having sexual contact with someone who has passed out, or having someone drugged or cognitively impaired sign over power of attorney. Only by placing myself in the position of the other, treating the other with the same respect that I would ask for in that situation, and displacing my own desires when challenged by the incapacity of the other to engage in consensual activity can any of us make ethical decisions in life at large. Ethics always requires judgment calls, and the parameters of what is being decided bear on this significantly. If the other person seems trashed but just wants to kiss and engage in a bit of mutual masturbation in the already consented-to space of the sex club, I don't ponder capacity to consent deeply because the activity is inconsequential. If the other wants anal sex without a condom (which is well outside of my sex-club repertoire, in any case), the consequences involving a decision-maker who is HIV+ are obviously much greater. In claiming the sex club as an always already ethical space, what I'm suggesting is that we remind ourselves of the very complexity of its ethicality. The best we can do as participants, HIV-awareness activists, and non-club-going commentators, is to embrace the mundane consequentiality of sex-club ethics in all of its imprecision and difficulty.

One of Archard's major areas of uncertainty is that of differential power relationships and their effect on the capacity to consent (1998: 55–65). Economic class or age differences in social relationships involving sexual activity can easily complicate an optimal dynamic of freely solicited and freely given consent. As we saw earlier, Walter uses his economic power to lure the unemployed into sexual complicity. His abuses, however, are limit cases; most situations involving "difference" are far less straightforward. In sex clubs, youth is often, though not always, power. Conventional attractiveness is often, though not always, power. Ethnic difference can be power. No one can guess what turns any other individual "on," so to speak, so power is never as simple as traditional models of social hierarchy and exploitation would figure for us. Being a wealthy, white middle-aged man is no particular advantage in a club where the $15 admission price is all that it takes to enter a zone where being young, even if poor, may make one the most desired partner of the evening.

Difference is not erased in sex clubs, but it is warped and can be manipulated in ways that may make them particularly appealing for individuals whose lives outside the club are not ones of privilege. Positive experiences in the club do not substitute for economic or racial justice outside of the club, but they do figure for all the club-goers a different social model from the one they live every day. As a space where often hidden or unexpressed desires are brought to the foreground, the sex club fractures the homogeneity of cultural norms regarding attractiveness as purveyed by advertising and other media. Outside of the club, chubbiness, slovenliness, hairiness, shortness, and geekiness all have their admirers too, but the sex club brings those real human differences into intensified and ecstatic (or at least orgasmic) relationship.

"What happens in the sex club, stays in the sex club"—that is, unless one's health status changes because of what happens there, or if one feels rejected or ugly (and leaves then with a diminished sense of selfhood and value), or if one of your students walks through the door and approaches you with a sly grin on his face. Then the boundaries disappear. The latter happened two times in the years I frequented LA sex clubs and instantly brought the artificiality of the consensual, "anonymous" space of the club into focus. I exited the club immediately in both cases because, however much we like to think that there are spaces apart from the real world of mundane human interaction and narrow sexual strictures, we carry our bodies and consciousnesses with us as we move across those spaces. Memories persist beyond the boundaries of the club. I would never be able to look at the same student again without the memory of the sexual encounter resurfacing, just as he would never be able to interact in class, in an examination, or in an office-hour conference without the knowledge of prior sexual activity affecting the interaction. The fiction of some instrumental erasure of what happens in the space "apart" is dangerous when one must confront the differential power relationships operant within the non-club world. I might add that this is just as true for nonsexual but still intensely social friendships that develop between students and professors. Call me a prude when it comes to my narrow limits on all forms of social interaction between faculty and students (as some have), but I can well maintain my sex radical agenda at the same time I consider myself a thorough professional at my job.

However, the rare case of a student or acquaintance walking into a club should not distract us in this discussion of the vast majority of the encounters that remain anonymous in the sense of having little impact on or reflection of interpersonal social knowledge outside of the club. That anonymity is one of the great assets to the experimentations and role-playings that can take place inside the club. The shy office assistant may suddenly find himself a subject of intense desire. The wealthy business-man finds himself marginalized and excluded from a dynamic of desire where money doesn't matter. The elderly man finds someone a third his age who has intense fantasies about a grandfatherly type and thereby rediscovers his own attractiveness. While communication through verbal or nonverbal cues is key to the negotiation of what will and will not happen between two or more people, oftentimes little personal informa-tion is exchanged. In a sense then, we find in such interactions a herme-neutic experience that is also an exercise in creative writing. We read the other but also actively create the narrative in which the other plays a role reflecting our fantasy life.

Martha Nussbaum, in an essay exploring oppressive and non-oppres-sive forms of objectification, asks skeptically, "[I]n the absence of any narrative history with the person, how can desire attend to anything else but the incidental, and how can one do more than use the body of the other as a tool of one's own states?" (1999: 237). We fill in those narra-tives and do not leave our ethical, concerned selves behind in sexual activities with strangers. We are certainly no more likely to use someone as a "tool" without regard for his or her desires, needs, and basic humanity when interacting sexually in anonymous circumstances than we are in anonymous business relationships; indeed, given the flesh-on-flesh contact, murmurs, and reciprocities in anonymous encounters, we are likely more solicitous and responsive than investment-fund managers and bankers ever are. Furthermore, the anonymity of some sexual liai-sons may free us to explore forms of exchange that are not allowed in daily lives in which we can be much more heavily scripted (as academic administrators, students, or bus drivers) than we are in anonymous encounters. Or, of course, it can free us to be inconsiderate jerks. But, potentially, in negotiating ways to give and receive pleasure in the club, one's fantasies fuse with those of the other, and new sources of excitement and different bodily sensations offer themselves.

While nonverbal communication may be the only form of conversation, in the strictest Gadamerian sense, that occurs, such a dynamic of mutually agreed-upon objectification is neither static nor is it inherently oppressive. Henning Bech, in his analysis of anonymous sexual encounters, has termed this a *"being-together"* that potentially "overstep[s] the border between one and the other" (1997: 113). Similarly Guy Hocquenghem speaks of the "disappearance of objects and subjects [in discovering] that in matters of sex everything is simply communication" (1993: 150). When I learn something about myself and my bodily responses, and, just as importantly, about how to give pleasure to another person, a Gadamerian, dialogic fusion of a sort occurs. I may be wholly objectifying the other as some figure drawn from my sexual fantasy storehouse—cute grocery clerk, geeky lab partner, gruff repairman—that may have absolutely nothing to do with the reality of his life. But he is doing the same with me, and, in negotiating what we can do for and with each other to satisfy mutually our fantasies, we blur the lines between "object" and "subject," however little we know about the reality of the other's life outside the club (it is hardly surprising that a "thank you" is often exchanged after a satisfying encounter—anonymous sex is usually very polite sex). Within the space of the club, this is equally true of the exhibitionistic and voyeuristic, where consent is given to watch or be watched simply in deciding whether to choose an encounter in an open, visible space or a darker, more private space. The ethics of the sex club demand that if two people choose to enter an alcove by themselves then I respect their choice of relative privacy, but if others choose to exhibit themselves and I wish to watch, that is still a fusion of desires that should challenge our concept of a simple subject–object relationship.

The fears that Walter from *My Secret Life* raises because of his monstrous behavior toward the disempowered are offset in the mutuality and exchange that goes on in sexual interrelationships every day and night. Just because we challenge our own boundaries and allow others to challenge us hardly means that we become abusers of others. We always have the choice of whether or not to act ethically as sexual beings, whether we are in a monogamous heterosexual relationship or in non-monogamous "queer" relationships. The latter is no more ethically charged or challenged than the former, just as marital rape is no doubt exponentially more common than nonconsensual sex in sex clubs.

Gadamerian musings

Gadamer, twice married but always silent on the subject of sex, would likely have been shocked by Walter's behavior or what happens on a Saturday night in an orgy room at a bathhouse. Yet that hardly matters. His body of philosophical hermeneutic theory still pertains. It challenges us with its implication of the ways that all human encounters can be figured as a quest for understanding and that incremental shifts through such interpersonal exchanges occur inexorably. Yes, sexuality and "sex" as a bodily activity have both powerful corporeal aspects/implications and powerful—overdetermined—cultural aspects/implications. The act of orgasm—that ecstatic shattering that Amber Hollibaugh finds so crucial for a life filled with hope and purpose—is the meeting point of a bodily slippage of control and a host of discourses that attempt to control that slippage's meanings. It is a fraught boundary.

Yet if we can theoretically (and practically, to the extent possible) suspend our allegiance to those overdetermining cultural impositions, then the control-shattering act of orgasm, whether in solitude, pairs, or groups, is no more a threat to social structures or a sense of general ethical responsibility than any other temporally limited dissolution of selfhood. We might find varying degrees of overlap with what happens when we eat a sumptuous meal (at that banquet of life), take a nap, or sneeze uncontrollably. As Walter asks above, what is the big difference between fucking and "chewing, drinking, spitting, snotting, urinating, farting?" All involve a bodily function—sometimes urgently enacted— that can impinge upon our full and awake consciousness, as well as the quickness of our responses or ability to respond instrumentally, but none so impairs our judgment that they are inherently ethics-challenged or a threat to a functioning society. Of course, people make stupid and ethically irresponsible (or worse) choices when they drive drunk or shoplift or otherwise give into "desires" that are usually contained with narrow social channels. Almost all of us, however, will negotiate responsibly our desires for food, wine/beer, and CDs at our local music store within an overall structure of respect for others with whom we are interacting and whose rights and needs challenge our own self-interest.

We live in a state of multiply layered consciousness as a matter of daily life. Sex is a subset of that daily life that demands equally its multiply layered ethical decision-making. Sexual diversity, as it includes nonmonogamous, anonymous, and fetishistic behaviors (among many others) needs to be so mundanely treated that the ethics of the sex club, the porn theatre, or the orgy are no more fraught than the ethics of the shopping center or the dance club. I can politely say "no" to someone who asks me to dance. I can politely say "no" to someone who invites me to participate in a multi-partnered sex scene. I can decide not to have that third glass of wine before driving home in my car. I can decide not to have anal intercourse without a condom. The lure of the latter may be greater than that of the former for some people (though the situation will be reversed for others), but in reading sexuality as simply one more text in a host of other mundane texts, we are encouraged to read its ethics as simply part and parcel of a broader ethics of daily life.

This making-ordinary approach to radical sexual practices, what Bech has termed "a huge *de-dramatization*" (1997: 209), may actually run counter to what some people find most productive of desire: the danger, the forbidden, the sense of transgression. And, yes, I'm sure some drinkers were disappointed with the end of Prohibition. Some pot smokers might be secretly saddened if marijuana is ever legalized. The breaking of the boundary can be pleasurable if one considers oneself a seeker of adventure, a different sort of person apart from mainstream and conformist types, a brave and trailblazing personality. Many of us have a little (or more than a little) Nietzsche in us.

I can only speak out of my own worldview. I would greatly prefer to live in a social environment where my desires—whatever they may be and so long as I conduct myself ethically—are simply considered my business and as inconsequential as the cuisine I prefer, though also perhaps as interesting to talk about and compare notes on as the cuisine I prefer. From my discovery of *The Happy Hooker* to the websites I may peruse later today, I love reading sexuality. I love reading Gadamer and George Eliot too. A good novel about a life of successes and failures, a new cookbook on an interesting cuisine, the elucidation of an interesting and useful new social theory, a detailed narrative about a different sexual possibility that I can try on imaginatively and perhaps try out corporeally—they really shouldn't be considered all that different. It is from that matter-of-factness about sexual diversity that we can tease out the ethical complications and demands posed by sexual interactions—whether paired, multi-partnered, or web-mediated.

If there is then an ethics of radical sexuality that I can offer from a reading of *My Secret Life* and my own sexual past it is one derived from the Gadamerian injunction to approach every dialogic encounter (which means every interpersonal encounter imaginable) as a learning opportunity that involves a critical attachment to the self as generated through the perspective of the other. This critical attachment does not mean denying, degrading, or doing violence to the self—we all must be self-confident enough to generate also the perspectives others require to learn—but it does mean questioning first, in every interaction, our own presuppositions as we render judgments and offer opinions.

That is what I believe we still have to learn from Gayle Rubin's decades-old work. Even as we continue to read and respond critically to the ethics-laden actions of others (and hold accountable in whatever way we can those who act abusively or insensitively), we should never fail to allow even the most disturbing narratives to disturb also our own sense of self-awareness and self-satisfaction. Gadamer reminds us that we have something to learn from every other being on this planet, even if the offered lesson is one about how necessary some boundaries are, or how some power-laden relationships should never involve sexual contact, or how general changes in social attitudes toward diverse sexual relationships can leave much still unaddressed in our problem-riddled world. Rubin confronts our panicky reaction to sexual diversity and asks instead for understanding. Even if we disagree with her reading of what constitutes benign variation, we are still left questioning "How do I know what I think I know?" and "How should I treat others given my awareness of my fallibility?" That uncertainty marks the starting point of a queer ethics of mutual consideration and delight.

Conclusion
How sex changes

Anyone who enjoys erotica (as I do) and who has kept for many years old magazines, videos, and novels (as I have) has easy access to evidence of just how significantly our sexual desires can change over long periods of time. Such changes are neither linear nor absolute; they are neither predictable nor reflective solely of broader fashion trends and image systems. Fashion does pertain, of course. When I glance at an old porn magazine or reread an erotic story from the 1980s that once sent electric jolts through my body, I often notice the temporal embeddedness of the language and imagery. Tube socks stand out in all their 1970s glory; the jargon and catchphrases of yesteryear often strike me as tired and slightly embarrassing. Gadamer reminds us that we always judge the past from the present, and if I no longer regularly see guys walking around with Shaun Cassidy-style feathered hair and wearing short shorts, I'll certainly react to their time-bound appearance in a film from thirty years ago. While there is no predicting the complexities of my or anyone else's range and peculiarities of desire (sometimes the very retro nature of the image may make it a turn-on), we all change in our perceptions of what is sexy, fresh, and exciting, even if we inevitably remember and continue to reference the past. No one's desires are frozen in time for the simple reason that the available language and image systems by which they are generated and expressed change inexorably.

Yet other things strike me as I glance at the old magazines and reread the porn novels from years or decades ago. My desires have shifted in ways that are unrelated to clothing trends and reigning pop icons. The S&M narratives that used to turn me on now leave me cold; I stopped buying them years ago. Moreover, I still remember well, looking through twenty-five-year-old magazines, which images excited me the most when they first appeared in the mail and which I ignored or rushed past. In the 1980s and into the 1990s I was obsessed with skinny, hairless, blond guys; I ignored chunkier bodies and found unattractive anyone with hairy legs or chests, though those body types were certainly well represented in the magazines themselves. Today, I look at the skinny blonds who used to catch my eye and feel completely uninterested, just as I am when seeing their offspring in today's twink magazines. The slightly stockier guy, with body hair, suddenly jumps out from the page even from a magazine twenty years old; the same type of guy is the one who rivets me today when I watch a new porn video. The Latino guy whom I breezed past when I first saw him in the 1980s now quickens my pulse. The tightly toned stomach of another guy whom I swooned over in the early 1990s now elicits a yawn, while the untoned torso of guy a few pages later seems natural and now intensely desirable.

It hardly matters why my own desires may have shifted in concert with the idiosyncrasies of my life: who I have dated or partnered with, how I have experienced my own body as it has aged, where I have lived, and who I see on the street every day. More important is the simple point that my desires have changed in significant ways, and that human sexual desire is surprisingly fluid when considered diachronically. If it were not, we would all develop crushes on twelve-year-olds, just as we did when we were twelve. What I will explore in the remaining pages of this book is how we might understand some of the mechanisms driving such change and how approaching change hermeneutically allows us to look toward a queerly changing future with eagerness and even optimism.

To make reference again to one of the focal texts of the preceding chapter, the change process is, for me, nowhere more apparent than in the dialogically hyperactive (even if few words are spoken there) venue of the sex club. In the microcosm of the sex club, the possibilities for exploring and gratifying desires that arise in new and surprising ways are unparalleled because of the very design and purpose of the venue itself. In a sense, it provided me with a laboratory of change possibilities. When someone offered to do something to me that I had never had done to me before—that had never even occurred to me—I could try it out immediately, for the sake of gratifying curiosity, whether or not it struck me as already inherently "desirable." If I did like it, then it became—unfailingly—a source of desire in future interactions. If I didn't like it, then it remained either something toward which I felt indifference or a new distaste. Yet until someone offered to do the previously unimagined "x" to me, I didn't even know if it was a source of pleasure and so had never desired it. The text of my own desires is therefore one that I did not write myself, nor was it written for me solely through some quasi-Freudian developmental process that ended in adolescence; it has been co-written with and overwritten repeatedly by innumerable authors (throughout my life and continuing to this day) who have augmented that text in generous and sometimes highly skillful ways. I owe those strangers, lovers, and friends enormous thanks for their acts of kindness and inventiveness and hope that I have returned their favors with equal enthusiasm and pleasurable effect.

My broader point from the previous chapter remains relevant here: That what happens in the sex club does not pertain only to the sex club, that the changes generated within the hothouse of the club are only intensified versions of those that all of us encounter as our desires shift and mutate over time and as our lives are lived in forms of verbal and nonverbal dialogue with that which surrounds us. My partner of many years has had enormous impact on my desires, as I have on his, as we have, over time, explored each other's bodies with patience and good humor. Similarly, and as mentioned earlier, the many places where I have lived and visited and the individuals who I have met there have left indelible marks on my desiring self. These were neither predictable nor were they wholly disconnected to conscious decisions that I made. Here, as elsewhere in my discussion, I emphasize that we can make self-aware choices in our dialogic interactions, affecting both their quantity and, one might say, quality. Simply put, the more we are willing and able to experiment and to allow ourselves to be vulnerable and look foolish before others (in other words, the more unlike David from *Giovanni's Room* we are), the more likely we are to discover new and powerful vectors of desire. Whether in a long-term monogamous relationship or in frequent orgiastic contact with anonymous fellow club-goers, we are unlikely to discover, for example, that a discrete, controlled form of pain—a fiercely pinched nipple or bitten earlobe—can be intensely exciting until someone offers it as an interpersonal experience and we accept the offer not knowing the result, or we experiment on ourselves after encountering the possibility through reading or otherwise processing someone else's sexual narrative. New encounters offer learning potentials that produce new desires.

The possibilities for such generative encounters are proliferating today as never before because of expanding access to the web. Granted, "seeing" is not precisely the same thing as body-to-body "doing," but it is a significant form of "doing" nevertheless. We should never define "sexuality" in the field of radical sexual or queer studies as solely that which involves genital or bodily contact. To do so would be to deny sexuality to anyone who has not "had sex" with another person, who is celibate or auto-erotic, or who for whatever reason has yet to act interpersonally on some of her or his most intense desires. My sexual hermeneutic response as I encounter images, narratives, or data on the screen is an active response. Processing what I see, hear, or read constitutes a dialogic encounter in which the horizon represented by/inherent within the position of the other meets, confronts, fuses with, and changes my own preconceptions and prejudices. My body responds sexually, affectively, and intellectually (and those are not discrete categories). My desires shift and accommodate (or do not) what I encounter; my horizon alters inevitably. Just as when I process any other text or engage inter-personally, I may or may not change significantly through the encounter, but I cannot leave precisely the same as I was before it occurred. The difference online is that the quantity and variety of possible encounters represents an intensification of the change mechanism for those whose lives involve erotic web-surfing, and there are significant aspects of agency involved in the number and variety of choices that we make online.

As a concrete example from my own media repertoire, when I visit a website such as www.xtube.com, I am immediately presented with a wide array of decisions to make that affect how and to what extent my erotic boundaries are challenged, though certainly they do not offer instrumental agency nor do they neatly contain my visual/aural encounters to that which is wholly predictable. Xtube is, as I write this, an open site, allowing anyone free access to an incredible quantity of erotic materials after passing through a simple portal that asks for confirmation that the visitor is over eighteen years of age. One can choose then to enter the site for "straight" content (that tab is accompanied by a smiley face), "gay" content (accompanied by a more broadly smiling face), or "both" content (accompanied by a wildly grinning face). After entering, one can peruse snippets of porn films that are available for purchase or thou-sands of uploaded videos from men and women showing an incredible variety of sex acts, fetish practices, teaser scenes, and monologues. Content is augmented minute by minute, so even if one stays on the site for only half an hour, one encounters many new videos and uploads as viewing possibilities.

Clearly one "chooses" the content that attracts one the most—if I am decidedly not into bondage and domination, I am unlikely to click on an icon to see a B&D short film—and therefore the possibilities for exploration and new exposures are limited by choices reflecting the tra-ditions that one carries within a body that has preexisting parameters of desire. However, the unpredictability of others' offered narratives and the availability of slightly different or tangentially related erotica, that falls almost but not quite within one's previous range of experience, makes the Xtube experience temporally dynamic. Unlike much previous media, such as packaged DVDs or bound magazines which clearly advertised and then carefully remained within their articulated bound-aries (no penises in *Playboy*, no contact between men in "lesbian" videos designed for heterosexual male viewers), boundaries abrade quickly on the web. On Xtube, even if I choose only straight content, bisexual videos showing male-on-male sexual contact are always offered as temptations. If I choose gay content, I'm still regularly offered choices that would lead me far astray. Given the opportunity to sample "MILF" porn (featuring mature women), I might click on it just to see if I like it. And I might be surprised that I do. My desire has shifted in concert with a set of decisions that I made, but did so in ways that I could not predict or fully control. Even when viewing a scene that promises to align precisely with desires that are predictable or traditional for me, I may find that the narrative takes a turn into something that I had never seen or desired before (someone suddenly enters dressed as a furry bunny—a "plushie"). I may respond with desire or I may quickly click to end the video (the sense memory of the smell and texture of synthetic fur from my childhood teddy bears completely kills my desire, I have discovered). But one cannot always predict where one's desires will go, how they will shift or expand, or how they might remain resilient through the experience of the banquet of sexual possibilities offered on a highly trafficked and content-rich site such as Xtube. And when one moves beyond Xtube and considers also the differently and variously active roles allowed by following links to chatrooms, avatar sites, and other venues for online encounters, the web presents us with a stunning new engine driving changes in innumerable individuals' sexualities, if censors do not eventually impede us.

Nevertheless, what remains true about even the newest and most dynamic forms of media-based sexual conversation is that our personal traditions and sedimented psyches will always have a slowing effect on any potentially radical outcome of encounters we may have. We do not suddenly jettison our old selves as we encounter new sexual horizons. I may suddenly find myself "into" MILF or DILF (daddy) porn but that has everything to do with a personal history and set of preexisting openings in the parameters of my desires that predated the encounter with the MILF snippet. We are not diachronically static, but neither are we subject to quick and radical breaks with the past. As this book has suggested from its opening chapter, the Gadamerian model offers us a way of understanding the incrementalism of such changes, as the past meets potential futures in the present. In allowing for this "situated knowing," as Lorraine Code terms it, we can appreciate Gadamer's utility "at a micropolitical level where acts of empowerment can initiate changes, however minuscule, in the social order, with incremental effects that extend beyond the places of their enactment" (2003: 34). Granted, MILF porn may not strike some people as micro-politically significant, but such an appraisal would depend wholly upon one's assessment of the "political" as it concerns age, for example. To my mind, any horizontal proliferation of desire possibilities, without value judgment or hierarchization (beyond Xtube's placement of "bisexual" content as the best choice of all), has a micropolitical and potentially macropolitical effect that I see as noteworthy. And Xtube is hardly alone in this cultural work. Rival website www.PornoTube.com operates in similarly unpredictable and proliferating fashion, though www.YouPorn.com has more heterosexual material than the other two. All, however, offer easy to access, free content that allows for anonymous experimentation and desire-altering slippages among previously sacrosanct categories. According to the web research firm Alexa (www.alexa.com), both YouPorn and Xtube are among the top 200 most-visited websites in the world, and both are in the top 100 in the USA. As I write this, Xtube is 83rd and YouPorn is 28th (for comparison, www.foxsports.com is 86th and www.washingtonpost.com is 97th). Those many millions of visits represent enormous potential for gradual shifts in erotic subjectivity.

My emphasis here on a queer sexual incrementalism runs athwart that of much recent work on queer temporality. The articulations of Judith Halberstam have been particularly useful and generative on this topic, even as they also warrant rejoinder and augmentation. In her *In a Queer Time and Place,* Halberstam pointedly reminds us that a queer temporality would avoid a reliance on hetero/repro-normative narratives of individual maturation and linear personal development: "Queer time," she says, "is a term for those specific models of temporality that emerge within postmodernism once one leaves the temporal frames of bourgeois reproduction and family, longevity, risk/safety, and inheritance" (Halberstam 2005: 6). Much of her focus is on a "mode of temporality that might arise out of an immersion in club cultures or queer sex cultures" (Halberstam 2005: 174), as she discusses her own experience of late nights spent at drag shows and music events. Hers is a version of a queer temporality that repudiates a narrative structure delineating what is "proper" for a forty-year-old, fifty-year-old, or sixty-year-old. As she notes in a contribution to a roundtable on the topic, "Queer time for me is [...] a way of being in the world and a critique of the careful social scripts that usher even the most queer among us through major markers of individual development and into normativity" (Dinshaw et al. 2007: 182). I commend that interrogation of narratives of aging and find much that is useful in a rethinking of when and how we are told to "mature."

Nevertheless, even as we bring powerful analytical tools to bear on those narratives of maturation and development, we are not beyond or outside of temporality. Annamarie Jagose in the same roundtable just mentioned, speaks to the general complexity of theorizing temporality when she asks,

> Rather than invoke as our straight guy a version of time that is always linear, teleological, reproductive, future oriented, what difference might it make to acknowledge the intellectual traditions in which time has also been influentially thought and experienced as cyclical, interrupted, multilayered, reversible, stalled—and not always in contexts easily recuperated as queer?
>
> (Dinshaw et al. 2007: 186–7)

I would add that there are many linearities and semi-linearities alongside our experiences of the nonlinear, and not all are reducible to the development narrative that Halberstam criticizes. We are never going to capture fully and accurately what temporality means; the best we can do is explore versions of temporality that correspond to our own queer experiences of time and change and that offer partial insights into how we might best, even if imperfectly, abet change.

My contribution here to the queer conversation on temporality is to point out the critical and political utility of appreciating specifically incremental change and recognizing the generative possibilities of horizons fusing and epistemological standpoints confronting one another, as offered through a wide range of interpersonal and mediated encounters. Halberstam is correct in pointing out the potential dynamism of dance/ performance club and urban sex subcultural life. It is equally true, however, that the normativities of the dance or sex club can be just as narrow and static as those of the church or PTA meeting. To revisit the same club over and over again is to discover that many patrons are not particularly interested in change. A club is a club because it has an identity, and a dance club's identity is not necessarily any more dynamic than that of one's parents' country club in the suburbs. One of the most poignant lessons of *Stone Butch Blues*, discussed in Chapter 3, is that Jess discovers her alternate family of Buffalo butches and femmes can be as racist and rigid as any family of bloodline rather than choice.

What I suggest here and throughout this book is that generative possibilities arise from any new encounters and excursions that take us outside of our own, even queer, safe zones. One name, besides Gadamer's, lacking from the discussion to date of queer temporalities is that of Louis Althusser, who famously suggests that we are "hailed" by ideology and come to recognize our selves through external ideological constructs which we internalize then as our "selves" (1971: 174–5). While recognizing the utility of the Althusserian model, Judith Butler and others have long critiqued the seemingly static nature of the image of a "hailing" that unilaterally determines one's subjectivity. Butler argues that "we might reread 'being' as precisely the potentiality that remains unexhausted by any particular interpellation" (1997: 131). What Butler does, in effect, is pluralize interpellation and uncouple it from a model of simple determination. This is also what Gadamerian hermeneutics leads us to do.

There is no one scene of ideological formation in our lives, captured so powerfully, if reductively, in the Althusserian image of a policeman calling out to us and eliciting a response that then defines us forever. We are not hailed once, we are hailed repeatedly, variously, and sometimes cacophonously in our lives, and we respond in variously active and passive ways. While I've never found a reference to Althusser in Gadamer's work, and only tangential ones in commentary on Gadamer, I suggest that every dialogic encounter, broadly defined as I have done so here, is a potential hailing. When I meet someone for the first time, visit a new website, read a book, open an email, or answer a telephone call, I encounter a worldview different from my own, with a set of differing ideologies, experiences, and values that can challenge the self-satisfaction of my perspective.

"Join us," says the email from the political action group; "here is what we stand for."

"Join me," says the MILF snippet; "you might like it."

"Listen to me," says the student, "I know some things about queer life in West Virginia that you do not."

To some, I say "yes," to others "maybe," and to others still "yuck, absolutely not," with my responses ranging from the overtly expressed and carefully argued, to the partially thought-out and imperfectly articulated, to the knee-jerk and rather stupid. Yet all are dialogic encounters that are the imperfect mechanism of personal and broader social change through the fusion possibilities that Gadamer discusses. The more, and more varied, the set of encounters that we seek out, take note of, and participate in with openness and intelligence, the more likely our own worldviews will be challenged and changed.

Yes, we carry with us always our inherited values, norms, psyches, and desires. Nothing that I am saying here is meant to deny the heavy weight of broad cultural and intensely personal tradition. As we age, certainly, we have many years and decades of sedimented interpellations that weigh upon our responses to any new hailing. I do not want to call this "maturation" of the sort that Halberstam rightly critiques; it is, however, the force of personal tradition that makes the response of a sixty-year-old to a new hailing different from that of a fifteen-year-old.

To revert to the Gadamerian metaphor, our horizons shift but we do not leave behind our past experiences and points of view. That lingering force of tradition is no cause for particular pessimism, simply an inevitable effect of time on the psyche. In fact, it should move us to even greater dialogic activity. The only mechanism for the disruption of heavily sedimented interpellations is through eager and vigorous encounters with difference. My horizon shifted when I threw myself into Los Angeles sex culture in the 1990s. It continues to shift significantly even in small-town West Virginia. When I go into the office of a legislator to lobby for a state employment nondiscrimination act and hear the point of view and about the concerns of that woman or man from a rural district—even as I voice also my own perspectives, values, and needs—a fusion occurs that should shift us both in our knowledge and understanding. When I visit a website that acquaints me with a different sexual practice than any I had previously experienced, my horizon shifts to accommodate at least the knowledge of it, even if it doesn't hail me successfully as a new devotee of it. When I let a student challenge my knowledge base about her life or his life in its queer complexity, across differences in age, ethnicity, or geographical location, my own worldview shifts and changes through the encounter.

Not all these encounters are ideological hailings, in the precise way that Althusser discussed, but they are engagements with belief systems that urge themselves upon us as potentially valid even if contextually rooted. We do not respond affirmatively to all of them; to many we may take vigorous exception, especially if they deny our humanity or right to read the books or explore the very websites that can be so generative. However, the fact remains that only through such encounters do we learn anything about our selves or our limitations. Only through an engagement with difference do we change.

Here, as earlier, the questions always are, how do we approach an encounter and how do we multiply and vary our encounters? A trip abroad, a visit to a new club, a conversation with a politician or student holding a significantly different point of view—all these are potentially life-changing experiences. Yet even in mentioning them as concrete examples, it is clear that they all also spring from a personal history, imagination, and worldview that reflects my life and position as a middle-class professor and political activist. How do we proliferate those possibilities beyond the academy and academic queer community?

I again return to the web as a site with extraordinary potential for general social change. While not everyone will own a personal computer, expanding numbers of people worldwide do have access to web cafés and computers in libraries and other sites. My utopian hope is that access to unfiltered, uncensored information will become a basic human right along with access to healthcare, shelter, food, and clean water. I needed that access when I was growing up in rural Alabama and did not have it, so was exceedingly lucky that I encountered Hollander when I did. She changed my worldview and my sexual selfhood. Similarly, sex will change in the future and for increasing numbers of people because of the web and to the extent that we make unrestricted web access an international human-rights priority. As I mentioned in my fourth chapter, this cannot and will not be a unidirectional overlay of Western notions of sexual identity on all other parts of the world. Global sexualities are already a pastiche, and that multiplicity will certainly increase.

I am not blind to the dangers of such new media. Misinformation abounds on the web; a critical hermeneutic approach to what we encounter there is vital. Abusive and exploitive encounters are also always possible, and they too must be energetically discussed in schools and families. Even so, unfettered access to the web is vital for everyone: for adolescents coming into their sense of sexuality and for adults as that sexuality continues to change. Most would agree that Xtube is unsuitable for thirteen- or fourteen-year-olds (though undoubtedly many have already visited the site); however, information about sex, sexuality, and sexual identity from a wide variety of viewpoints is critical for thirteen- and fourteen-year-olds. Only thereby is there any hope of disrupting the rigid, deadly, and destructive polarities of hetero/homo as a naturalized, hierarchized binary. I am optimistic that sex is already changing because most adolescents today know how to surf the web effectively with and around filters and other censoring mechanisms. Sex will continue to change because any adult with interest in rethinking her or his assumptions about sexuality now has access to a myriad of possibilities online for discovering different viewpoints and ways of being in the world. Conservative politicians and religious leaders are right to worry about the effect of the web on young and old alike. Sex will change because of it.

It can do so even more rapidly if we approach every encounter with the Gadamerian attitude of remaining critical, open, and eager. The Gadamerian requisite is to question: What can I learn from this? How does the encounter highlight my own limitations? That attitude of humility and curiosity serves us well when we are speaking among ourselves as queer intellectuals, when we are speaking to political interlocutors holding very different belief systems, when we as adolescents or adults are looking for answers about possibilities for sexual identification and affiliation, and when we travel through this queer world and hopefully treat others with the inherent respect that can only derive from an acknowledgment of our own imperfect knowledge. This does not mean ignoring or apologizing for racism, sexism, and homophobia on the parts of our interlocutors. It does mean however working to understand them so we can respond effectively. We are all capable, or should be capable, of speaking effectively out of our own subject positions while allowing those positions to shift as they encounter the words and beliefs of others. Change occurring from those interactions will never be domino-like. The domino metaphor, as deployed by conservatives, is one that arises from the same belief in quick and radical alteration that animated much of early queer theory itself. Yet change can be radical even if it is not quick. Both active choices and chance-driven occurrences lead to changes in our lives and desires that are unpredictable but exciting for that very reason. There is no reason for panic, only for cautious optimism that there are broader sociocultural forces at work already that are trending toward a proliferation of new and different sexual subject positions available to greater numbers of individuals within the Anglo-American cultural sphere, as well as across the globe. My hope here is that all of us on the sexual "left" will embrace and further a process of thoughtful and eagerly debated proliferation.

Indeed, we must embrace politics in all of its messiness and potential for disappointment. A belief in instrumental agency and an expectation of quick results are deadly. If, as several commentators including Lauren Berlant (whom I quoted in my introduction) and Ann Cvetkovich have suggested, queer theory is suffering from a "'political depression,' the sense that customary forms of political response, including direct action and critical analysis are no longer working either to change the world or to make us feel better" (Cvetkovich 2007: 460), then we need a more modest, if incrementally ambitious, strategy. Speaking out, rather than to ourselves, is key here. If we are going to avoid the dominance of the multinational media conglomerates in driving the subject positions offered individuals worldwide through advertising campaigns, then we queer intellectuals need to be a vital part of the conversation. The same is true if we wish to counter the homo-normative voices of the gay- and lesbian-rights organizations that make marriage the holy grail of all political activism on the left. We cannot opt out of a conversation that must include concrete projections, well-articulated agendas, and energizing, if always provisional, utopian articulations. Those vocalizations must enter the broad conversation as alternatives to media images of happy consuming lesbians and blissfully married middle-class gay men. Only through active conversational input of the most concrete sorts are we able to counter the heavy weight of the conventional and depressing images and projections of others, some of whom even think of themselves as sexual progressives.

This is not instrumental agency, but it is a modest form of influence. My hope is that we as radical sexual theorists and practitioners will embrace that modesty, appreciate the incrementalism that is the substructure of social change, relish the heavily compromised agency of all intellectual input, and find a praxis that is appropriate for 2010 and the decades beyond. I hold no nostalgia for an early queer praxis that was driven by the HIV-related deaths of innumerable friends and political allies. My concern is with the now and the to-be, while not ignoring the past as it forms the discursive base matter of our desires, thoughts, and images. Our own traditions demand the respectful and carefully critical attention that Gadamer reminds us is necessary as we forge any future-oriented agenda. That engaging mix of past, present, and projected futures is the conversational dynamic that should be our basis for optimism.

The more hetero the conversation, the better it is. The same voices spouting variations on the same themes and theoretical perspectives lead to an implicit normativity of their own. I am much more encouraged politically and intellectually by the openness evident in a recent issue of the journal *Radical History Review* on the topic of "Queer Futures" (winter 2008) with its inclusion of activist voices and nonacademic perspectives than I am with many of the recent publications coming out of the cultural studies/queer theory mainstream. I have quoted many voices throughout this book—devoted as it is to conversation as a practice and requisite for change—and I want to invoke one more here in my final pages.

Mattilda Bernstein Sycamore, a transgender San Francisco-based author/activist whom I quoted in my second chapter, participated in a long and revealing interview in that issue of *Radical History Review,* recounting what happened after she was invited to participate in an academic queer-studies conference. In attending it she was shocked at the group-think that dominated the event. Eager to challenge her fellow queers on the implicit "nationalism, racism, classism, patriotism, consumerism, militarism, patriarchy, imperialism, misogyny" (Ruiz 2008: 238) that too often accompanies homo-normative practices in both the academic and activist worlds, she hoped at the conference to "stimulate discussion" and "engage in [a] conversation about appropriation" (2008: 244). In her words,

> I talked about what I call "trickle-down academia," the process by which academics appropriate anything they can get their hands on and then claim to have invented it. What was fascinating was that people [...] did *not* want to engage in conversation. What they wanted to do was to shut us up. I had one academic start screaming at me, "You are just like Cheney!" Of all the silencing lines,

implying that by critiquing the academy we were furthering the goals of the Christian Right because the Christian Right is anti-academic! Therefore, all people who are critiquing academia are equivalent to the Christian Right. There were a couple of famous academics that got up and were screaming. [...] The people who were yelling were so concerned with their credibility and being perceived as outsider or radical academics that they didn't know what to do with us.

(Ruiz 2008: 244)

Obviously, the conversation ended there, though it continues more broadly as I write this and in two of Sycamore's recent books (*That's Revolting* and *Nobody Passes*), where she discusses the incident. And while Sycamore's perspective is only one of many concerning what happened at the conference in question, I have seen innumerable versions of the same dynamic in my many years in the field of queer theory. Queer academic egos can lead to violent rhetorical responses to differing perspectives, effectively ending conversations and maintaining a self-serving and deadly uniformity. Nothing about the scene described above, or similar ones I've witnessed before, fulfills any of the basic Gadamerian requisites for self-questioning and humility as part of a vibrant conversational dynamic. Perhaps that is why Gadamer is never referenced; he would remind queer theorists that sometimes they just need to shut up and listen to those beyond their small circle of academic allies and repeat interlocutors.

In Hiram Perez's words, queer theory should give up its "property claims demarcating intellectual territory" and "interrogat[e] its own capacity to listen imaginatively" (Perez 2005: 179). So let yourself be challenged. Come with me to the West Virginia state capitol and talk with closeted queer legislators who fear exposure but who nevertheless can be tactically sophisticated allies. Better yet—visit your own politicians in their offices, talk with them, and listen to them. Talk and listen to Log Cabin Republicans and closeted queer members of the armed services. Talk and listen to activists who do not always understand where academics "are coming from." Try to see the world through the other's eyes, acknowledge her or his hardships, express your perspectives vigorously but listen as carefully as you articulate. Invite into the conversation transgender activists, activists of color, rural and suburban queers, religious queers, married and parenting queers. Some will be living lives that reflect ideologies you will find worthy of thoughtful challenge. Our lives in their complexities and distinctions will not fuse well with those of many interlocutors, yet our careful participation in the conversations that follow is the only mechanism by which others will change. Our careful listening is the only mechanism by which we will change. I may be an educator by profession, but my first responsibility as a public intellectual and activist is to listen.

I return to Gadamer now at his life's end. On his 102nd birthday, he offered a few words to newspaper reporters, repeating what he called his only firm belief, that "people cannot live without hope; that is the only thesis I would defend without any restriction" (Grondin 2003: 335). Our hope, which should enliven our continued work toward our many desirably queer futures, can derive from the potentials inherent in the learning process itself, in which we still retain confidence, whether we fully admit it or not. If we did not believe in firm and fundamental ways in which people learn and change over time, no educator reading this book would ever enter a classroom and expect anything useful to happen there. All of us live change every day, and for that reason I am as optimistic as I have ever been about the future of queer sexualities, and I am still cautiously optimistic about the future of "queer theory," to the extent that its practitioners will *embrace the future*. To paraphrase Auntie Mame, we should all be talking, listening, eating, and sharing at the banquet of life, a banquet of differing perspectives, ideas, lifestyles, desires, images, hopes, and fears. That banquet is not only one of sexual and sensual pleasures, it is also one of narrative, conversational, political, and intellectual pleasures derived from the very variety of the encounters—the more varied, the better.

Now what do you have to say?

Bibliography

Ahmed, Sara (2006) *Queer Phenomenology: Orientations, Objects, Others,* Durham, NC: Duke University Press.

Alexander, Thomas (1997) "Eros and Understanding: Gadamer's Aesthetic Ontology of the Community," in Lewis Edwin Hahn (ed.), *The Philosophy of Hans-Georg Gadamer,* Chicago, Ill.: Open Court Press, pp. 323–45.

Althusser, Louis (1971) *Lenin and Philosophy and Other Essays,* New York: Monthly Review Books.

Altman, Dennis (2001) *Global Sex,* Chicago, Ill.: University of Chicago Press.

Archard, David (1998) *Sexual Consent,* Boulder, Col.: Westview Press.

Baldwin, James (2000) *Giovanni's Room,* New York: Delta.

Bech, Henning (1997) *When Men Meet: Homosexuality and Modernity,* trans. Teresa Mesquit and Tim Davies, Chicago, Ill.: University of Chicago Press.

Beck, Ulrich and Elisabeth Beck-Gernsheim (1995) *The Normal Chaos of Love,* trans. Mark Ritter and Jane Wiebel, Malden, Mass.: Blackwell Publishers.

Berlant, Lauren (2007) "Starved," *South Atlantic Quarterly,* 106 (3): 433–44.

Binnie, Jon (2004) *The Globalization of Sexuality,* London: Sage.

Bright, Susie (1999) *Full Exposure: Opening Up to Sexual Creativity and Erotic Expression,* New York: Harper Collins.

Butler, Judith (1993) *Bodies That Matter: On the Discursive Limits of "Sex,"* London and New York: Routledge.

—— (1997) *The Psychic Life of Power: Theories in Subjection,* Stanford, Calif.: Stanford University Press.

—— (1999) *Gender Trouble: Feminism and the Subversion of Identity,* 10th anniversary edn, London and New York: Routledge.

—— (2004) *Undoing Gender,* London and New York: Routledge.

—— (2005) *Giving an Account of Oneself,* New York: Fordham University Press.

Chasin, Alexandra (2000) *Selling Out: The Gay and Lesbian Movement Goes to Market,* Basingstoke: Palgrave.

Code, Lorraine (2003) "Introduction: Why Feminists Do Not Read Gadamer," in Lorraine Code (ed.), *Feminist Interpretations of Hans-Georg Gadamer,* University Park, Pa.: Pennsylvania State University Press, pp. 1–36.

Cruz-Malavé, Arnaldo and Martin F. Manalansan (2002) "Introduction: Dissident Sexualities/Alternative Globalisms," in Arnaldo Cruz-Malavé and Martin F. Manalansan (eds), *Queer Globalizations: Citizenship and the Afterlife of Colonialism*, New York: New York University Press, pp. 1–10.

Cvetkovich, Ann (2007) "Public Feelings," *South Atlantic Quarterly*, 106 (3): 459–68.

Dallmayr, Fred R. (1989) "Prelude: Hermeneutics and Deconstruction: Gadamer and Derrida in Dialogue," in Diane P. Michelfelder and Richard E. Palmer (eds), *Dialogue and Deconstruction: The Gadamer-Derrida Encounter*, Albany, NY: State University of New York Press, pp. 75–92.

Dean, Tim (2000) *Beyond Sexuality*, Chicago, Ill.: University of Chicago Press.

Delany, Samuel R. (1988) *The Motion of Light in Water: Sex and Science Fiction Writing in the East Village, 1957–1965*, New York: Arbor House.

—— (1999) *Times Square Red, Times Square Blue*, New York: New York University Press.

de Lauretis, Teresa (1994) "Habit Changes," *differences*, 6 (2/3): 296–313.

Derrida, Jacques (2007) *Learning to Live Finally: The Last Interview*, trans. Pascale-Anne Brault and Michael Naas, Hoboken, NJ: Melville House Publishing.

Dinshaw, Carolyn, Edelman, Lee, Ferguson, Roderick, Freccero, Carla, Freeman, Elizabeth, Halberstam, Judith, Jagose, Annamarie, Nealon, Christopher, and Nguyen Tan Hoang (2007) "Theorizing Queer Temporalities: A Roundtable Discussion," *GLQ*, 13 (2–3): 177–95.

Dolan, Jill (2005) *Utopia in Performance: Finding Hope at the Theater*, Ann Arbor, Mich.: University of Michigan Press.

Drucker, Peter (2000) "Introduction: Remapping Sexualities," in Peter Drucker (ed.), *Different Rainbows*, London: Gay Men's Press, pp. 9–41.

Duggan, Lisa (2003) *The Twilight of Equality? Neoliberalism, Cultural Politics, and the Attack on Democracy*, Boston, Mass.: Beacon Press.

Earl, Robert, dir. (1986) *Bi-Ceps: An Incredible Bisexual Experience*, Los Angeles, Calif.: LA Video.

Edelman, Lee (2004) *No Future: Queer Theory and the Death Drive*, Durham, NC: Duke University Press.

Eng, David L., with Judith Halberstam and José Esteban Muñoz, (2005) "Introduction: What's Queer About Queer Studies Now?" *Social Text*, 23 (3/4): 1–17.

Family Watch International (2007) Family Policy Brief, available at http://www.familywatchinternational.org/fwi/yogyakarta.pdf (accessed July 29, 2008).

Feinberg, Leslie (2003) *Stone Butch Blues*, Los Angeles, Calif.: Alyson.

Foucault, Michel (1990) *The History of Sexuality, Volume 1: An Introduction*, trans. Robert Hurley, New York: Vintage.

Gadamer, Hans-Georg (1985) *Philosophical Apprenticeships*, trans. Robert R. Sullivan, Cambridge, Mass.: MIT Press.

—— (1986) *The Idea of the Good in Platonic-Aristotelian Philosophy*, trans. P. Christopher Smith, New Haven, Conn.: Yale University Press.

—— (1989) "Destruktion and *Deconstruction*," trans. Geoff Waite and Richard Palmer, in Diane P. Michelfelder and Richard E. Palmer (eds), *Dialogue and*

Deconstruction: The Gadamer-Derrida Encounter, Albany, NY: State University of New York Press, pp. 102–13.

——— (2001) *Gadamer in Conversation: Reflections and Commentary,* ed. and trans. Richard E. Palmer, New Haven, Conn.: Yale University Press.

——— (2003) *Truth and Method,* trans. Joel Weinsheimer and Donald G. Marshall, 2nd edn, New York: Continuum.

——— (2006) "Rhetoric, Hermeneutics, and the Critique of Ideology: Metacritical Comments on *Truth and Method,*" in Kurt Müller-Vollmer (ed.), *The Hermeneutics Reader,* New York: Continuum, pp. 274–92.

Garber, Linda (2001) *Identity Poetics: Race, Class and the Lesbian-Feminist Roots of Queer Theory,* New York: Columbia University Press.

Giddens, Anthony (1992) *The Transformation of Intimacy: Sexuality, Love and Eroticism in the Late Modern Age,* Stanford, Calif.: Stanford University Press.

Goodyear, Dana (2006) "The Searchers," *The New Yorker,* September 2, pp. 62–71.

Grondin, Jean (2003) *Hans-Georg Gadamer: A Biography,* trans. Joel Weinsheimer, New Haven, Conn.: Yale University Press.

Grosz, Elizabeth (1994) *Volatile Bodies: Toward a Corporeal Feminism,* Bloomington, Ind.: Indiana University Press.

Halberstam, Judith (2005) *In a Queer Time and Place: Transgender Bodies, Subcultural Lives,* New York: New York University Press.

Halley, Janet and Andrew Parker (2007) "Introduction," *South Atlantic Quarterly,* 106 (3): 421–32.

Hall, Donald E. (2003) *Queer Theories,* Basingstoke: Palgrave.

——— (2004) *Subjectivity,* London and New York: Routledge.

Halperin, David M. (1995) *Saint Foucault: Towards a Gay Hagiography,* Oxford: Oxford University Press.

——— (2007) *What Do Gay Men Want? An Essay on Sex, Risk, and Subjectivity,* Ann Arbor, Mich.: University of Michigan Press.

Hekman, Susan (2003) "The Ontology of Change: Gadamer and Feminism," in Lorraine Code (ed.), *Feminist Interpretations of Hans-Georg Gadamer,* University Park, Pa.: Pennsylvania State University Press, pp. 181–202.

Henderson, Mae G. (1992) "Speaking in Tongues: Dialogics, Dialectics, and the Black Woman Writer's Literary Tradition," in Judith Butler and Joan W. Scott (eds), *Feminists Theorize the Political,* London and New York: Routledge, pp. 144–66.

——— (2005) "James Baldwin's *Giovanni's Room:* Expatriation, 'Racial Drag,' and Homosexual Panic," in E. Patrick Johnson and Mae G. Henderson (eds), *Black Queer Studies,* Durham, NC: Duke University Press, pp. 298–322.

Hicklin, Aaron (2007) "Editor's Letter," *Out,* August, p. 16.

Hollander, Xaviera (2002) *The Happy Hooker: My Own Story,* 30th anniversary edn, New York: Regan Books/Harper Collins.

Hocquenghem, Guy (1993) *Homosexual Desire,* trans. Daniella Dangoor, Durham, NC: Duke University Press.

Hollibaugh, Amber (2000) *My Dangerous Desires: A Queer Girl Dreaming Her Way Home,* Durham, NC: Duke University Press.

Jagose, Annamarie (1996) *Queer Theory: An Introduction,* New York: New York University Press.

Kapuściński, Ryszard (2007) "The Open World," trans. Klara Glowczewska, *The New Yorker,* February 5, pp. 58–65.

Kincaid, James (ed.) (1996) *My Secret Life: An Erotic Diary of Victorian London,* Anon., New York: Signet.

Locke, John (1975) *An Essay Concerning Human Understanding,* ed. Peter Nidditch, Oxford: Oxford University Press.

Lowe, E. J. (1995) *Locke on Human Understanding,* London and New York: Routledge.

Manalansan, Martin F. (1997) "In the Shadows of Stonewall: Examining Gay Transnational Politics and the Diasporic Dilemma," in Lisa Lowe and David Lloyd (eds), *The Politics of Culture in the Shadow of Capital,* Durham, NC: Duke University Press, pp. 485–505.

Manson, Marilyn, with Neil Strauss, (1998) *The Long Hard Road Out of Hell,* New York: Harper Collins.

Marcus, Stephen (1964) *The Other Victorians: A Study of Sexuality and Pornography in Mid-Nineteenth-Century England,* New York: Basic Books.

Mburu, John (2000) "Awakenings: Dreams and Delusions of an Incipient Lesbian and Gay Movement in Kenya," in Peter Drucker (ed.), *Different Rainbows,* London: Gay Men's Press, pp. 179–92.

Mejía, Max (2000) "Mexican Pink," in Peter Drucker (ed.), *Different Rainbows,* London: Gay Men's Press, pp. 43–56.

Meštrović, Stjepan (1998) *Anthony Giddens: The Last Modernist,* London and New York: Routledge.

Michelfelder, Diane P. and Richard E. Palmer (1989) *Dialogue and Deconstruction: The Gadamer-Derrida Encounter,* Albany, NY: State University of New York Press.

Miller, J. Hillis, with Manuel Asensi (1999) *Black Holes, J. Hillis Miller; or, Boustrophedonic Reading,* Stanford, Calif.: Stanford University Press.

Müller-Vollmer, Kurt (2006) "Introduction: Language, Mind, and Artifact" in Kurt Müller-Vollmer (ed.), *The Hermeneutics Reader,* New York: Continuum, pp. 1–53.

Muñoz, José Esteban (2002) "The Future in the Present: Sexual Avant-gardes and the Performance of Utopia," in Donald E. Pease and Robyn Wiegman (eds), *The Future of American Studies,* Durham, NC: Duke University Press.

—— (2006) "Thinking Beyond Antirelationality and Antiutopianism in Queer Critique," *PMLA,* 121 (3): 825–6.

—— (2007) "Queerness as Horizon: Utopian Hermeneutics in the Face of Gay Pragmatism," in George Haggarty and Molly McGarry (eds), *A Companion to Lesbian, Gay, Bisexual, Transgender, and Queer Studies,* Malden, Mass.: Blackwell, pp. 452–63.

Nietzsche, Friedrich (1966) *Beyond Good and Evil: Prelude to a Philosophy of the Future,* trans. Walter Kaufmann, New York: Vintage Press.

—— (1969) *On the Genealogy of Morals and Ecce Homo,* trans. Walter Kaufmann, New York: Vintage Press.

Nussbaum, Martha (1999) "Objectification," in *Sex and Social Justice,* Oxford: Oxford University Press.

Perez, Hiram (2005) "You Can Have My Brown Body, and Eat It Too!" *Social Text,* 23 (3/4): 171–92.

Puar, Jasbir K. (2005) "Queer Times, Queer Assemblages," *Social Text,* 23 (3/4): 121–39.

Ricoeur, Paul (1974) "The Tasks of the Political Educator," in *Political and Social Essays,* ed. David Stewart and Joseph Bien, Athens, Ohio: Ohio University Press, pp. 271–93.

—— (1986) *Lectures on Ideology and Utopia,* ed. George H. Taylor, New York: Columbia University Press.

—— (1991a) "The Conflict of Interpretations: Debate with Hans-Georg Gadamer, in Mario Valdés (ed.), *A Ricoeur Reader: Reflection and Imagination,* Toronto: University of Toronto Press.

—— (1991b) *From Text to Action: Essays in Hermeneutics II,* trans. Kathleen Blamey and John B. Thompson, Evanston, Ill.: Northwestern University Press.

—— (1991c) "Life: A Story in Search of a Narrator," in Mario Valdés (ed.), *A Ricoeur Reader: Reflection and Imagination,* Toronto: University of Toronto Press, pp. 425–37.

—— (1992) *Oneself as Another,* trans. Kathleen Blamey, Chicago, Ill.: University of Chicago Press.

Rubin, Gayle (1993) "Thinking Sex: Notes for a Radical Theory of the Politics of Sexuality," in Henry Abelove, Michele Aina Barale, and David Halperin (eds), *The Lesbian and Gay Studies Reader,* London and New York: Routledge, pp. 3–44.

Ruiz, Jason (2008) "The Violence of Assimilation: An Interview with Mattilda aka Matt Bernstein Sycamore," *Radical History Review,* 100 (winter): 237–48.

Santiago, Silviano (2002) "The Wily Homosexual (First—and Necessarily Hasty—Notes)," in Arnaldo Cruz-Malavé and Martin F. Manalansan (eds), *Queer Globalizations: Citizenship and the Afterlife of Colonialism,* New York: New York University Press, pp. 13–19.

Sedgwick, Eve Kosofsky (1997) "Paranoid Reading and Reparative Reading; or, You're So Paranoid, You Probably Think This Introduction is About You," in Eve Kosofsky Sedgwick (ed.), *Novel Gazing. Queer Readings In Fiction,* Durham, NC: Duke University Press, pp. 1–37.

Sender, Katherine (2004) *Business, Not Politics: The Making of the Gay Market,* New York: Columbia University Press.

Simms, Karl (2003) *Paul Ricoeur,* London and New York: Routledge.

Sinfield, Alan (2004) *On Sexuality and Power,* New York: Columbia University Press.

Sloterdijk, Peter (1987) *Critique of Cynical Reason,* trans. Michael Elred, Minneapolis, Minn.: University of Minnesota Press.

Sprinkle, Annie (2005) *Dr. Sprinkle's Spectacular Sex: Make Over Your Love Life with One of the World's Great Sex Experts,* New York: Tarcher/Penguin.

Strongman, Roberto (2002) "Syncretic Religion and Dissident Sexualities," in Arnaldo Cruz-Malavé and Martin F. Manalansan (eds), *Queer Globalizations:*

Citizenship and the Afterlife of Colonialism, New York: New York University Press, pp. 176–92.

Sycamore, Mattilda Bernstein (ed.) (2006) *Nobody Passes: Rejecting the Rules of Gender and Conformity,* Emeryville, Calif.: Seal Press.

—— (2008) *That's Revolting: Queer Strategies for Resisting Assimilation,* rev. edn, Brooklyn: Soft Skull Press.

Taylor, Charles (1989) *Sources of the Self: The Making of the Modern Identity,* Cambridge, Mass.: Harvard University Press.

Tompkins, Jane and Gerald Graff (2001) "Can We Talk?" in Donald E. Hall (ed.), *Professions: Conversations on the Future of Literary and Cultural Studies,* Urbana, Ill.: University of Illinois Press, pp. 21–36.

Turner, William B. (2000) *A Critical Genealogy of Queer Theory,* Philadelphia, Pa.: Temple University Press.

Vasterling, Veronica (2003) "Postmodern Hermeneutics? Toward a Critical Hermeneutics," in Lorraine Code (ed.), *Feminist Interpretations of Hans-Georg Gadamer,* University Park, Pa.: Pennsylvania State University Press, pp. 149–80.

Warner, Michael (1993) "Introduction," in Michael Warner (ed.), *Fear of a Queer Planet: Queer Politics and Social Theory,* Minneapolis, Minn.: University of Minnesota Press.

Wiseman, Jay (1998) *SM 101: A Realistic Introduction,* 2nd edn, Emeryville, Calif.: Greenery Press.

Wright, Kathleen (2003) "(En)gendering Dialogue Between Gadamer's Hermeneutics and Feminist Thought," in Lorraine Code (ed.), *Feminist Interpretations of Hans- Georg Gadamer,* University Park, Pa.: Pennsylvania State University Press, pp. 39–55.

Yogyakarta Principles (2007), available at http://www.yogyakartaprinciples.org (accessed July 29, 2008).

Ziarek, Ewa Plonowska (2001) *An Ethics of Dissensus: Postmodernity, Feminism, and the Politics of Radical Democracy,* Stanford, Calif.: Stanford University Press.

Index